THE PACIFIC COAST
RHODODENDRON
STORY

Portland Chapter
American Rhododendron Society Committee

Mike Stewart
Ted Van Veen
Eleanor Stubbs
Dr. Dave Goheen
Dr. Bob Ticknor

THE PACIFIC COAST RHODODENDRON STORY

The Hybridizers, Collectors and Gardens

Sonja Nelson

with the
Portland Chapter
American Rhododendron Society

BINFORD & MORT PUBLISHING

PORTLAND, OREGON

The Pacific Coast Rhododendron Story:
The Hybridizers, Collectors and Gardens

Printed in the United States of America

Library of Congress Catalog Card Number: 2001087902

ISBN 0-8323-0537-5
ISBN 0-8323-0536-7 pbk

First Edition 2001

Front Cover Photo: Clayoquot Sound from Ken & Dot Gibson's Garden, Tofino, BC by Ray Talbot
Back Cover Photo: Crystal Springs Rhododendron Garden, Portland, Oregon by Bill Ferguson

Many thanks to the following for their generous financial support in the publishing of this book.

Sig & Mildred Berthelsdorf
Forrest & Rosemary Bump
Dick & Karen Cavender
Ed & Fran Egan
Robert Franz
Steve Hopkins
Peter Kendall
Alfred Martin
Herb & Betty Spady
Mike & Maria Stewart
Art & Eleanor Stubbs
Ted & Fran Van Veen
Harvey Welch
Franklin H. West
Philip & Consuelo Zeller

CONTENTS

PREFACE

The project of documenting the story of those who began the collecting and hybridizing of rhodondrons on the West Coast of the United States and Canada began some eight years ago. The Portland Chapter of the American Rhododendron Society at that time was preparing to host its 50th Anniversary Celebration Conference in Portland, Oregon. We had planned to produce a small book for the conference that would document the efforts of those in the West who had been the major hybridizers from our area. As the project proceeded, we realized that the book should be expanded to cover as many of the collectors, hybridizers and public gardens as possible from California through Western Canada. It became evident that we had a very important responsibility in capturing this history before it became even more difficult to collect and document. Little did we know then that the task of collecting biographical information, historical pictures, and writing the text would involve so many years of work.

As the title page suggests, this book is not meant to be just a list of hybrids and their respective parentages, but rather the "story" of those people who have a passion for growing, collecting and hybridizing this most beautiful plant, rhododendron. It is a story that begins with the very discovery of *R. macrophyllum*, and continues to the present. Along the way we discovered that just as rhododendrons have such a wide range of variety, form, texture and color, those who created them have just as colorful and varied personalities.

Our research started years ago with video and audio taping several discussions with small groups of "old-timers" including some charter members of the American Rhododendron Society. After much discussion pertaining to the more serious nature of how rhododendrons got their start in the West, the meetings would generally digress to "reminiscing" about old acquaintances and fellow rhododendron hybridizers; who they were most influenced by, and to whom they passed on their knowledge; what their focus in hybridizing was, and where they traveled to collect their pollen and seed. Their stories are as varied as their plants, and the results of their collecting and hybridizing are both beautiful and fascinating.

We were fortunate that most of our committee of researchers have, shall I say, "been around a while." The committee included Mike Stewart, Ted Van Veen, Eleanor Stubbs, Dr. Dave Goheen and Dr. Bob Ticknor. Their dedication and personal knowledge of those who have come before us was vast, and proved to be invaluable. In the first couple of years, Clarence Barrett did a fair amount of collecting information and writing, and should be acknowledged for his contribution. During the last two years, Sonja Nelson has written the final version as you see it in this book.

After Dr. Franklin West from the East wrote *Hybrids and Hybridizers*, he remarked that the West coast should produce such a book. The challenge finally has been met. The Portland Chapter of the American Rhododendron Society is proud to present this historical document to you, in hopes that it will further your knowledge and enjoyment of our beautiful and beloved rhododendron.

Mike Stewart
American Rhododendron Society
Western Vice President

ACKNOWLEDGMENTS

Our deep gratitude goes to those who contributed the historical data, biographical information and pictures which made this book possible: Ted Anderson, Jim Barlup, Clarence Barrett, Gwen Bell, Warren Berg, Emma and Tom Bowhan, Ben Briggs, Ned Brockenbrough, Edith Brydon, Lansing and Eleanor Bulgin, Frances Burns, Cliff Cannon, James Caperci, Dick and Karen Cavender, Bill Dale, Joe Davis, Dot Dunstan, James Elliot, Walt Elliot, Ed and Fran Egan, Jean Falotico, Frank Fujioka, Bob George, Ken and Dot Gibson, Harold Greer, Garda Griswold, Bill Guttormsen, Pat Halligan, Honoré Hacanson, Carl G. Heller, John Henny, Gerald Heriot, Lillian Hodgson, Harold A. Johnson, Clive Justice, Laura Kentala, Harold Krug, Jack Lofthouse, Donald and Eleanor McClure, Mike McCullough, Ernie Metcalfe, Fred and Jean Minch, Bill Moynier, Frank Mossman, Jay Murray, Bernard Nelson, Lloyd and Edna Newcomb, Julius Nuccio, Carl and Linda Nys, Kristi O'Donnell, Norman Todd, Ed Parker, Don and Dorothy Patrick, Eleanor Philp, Lawrence Pierce, Roy Preston, Bob Rhodes, Charles Richards, Michael Robert, Bill Robinson, Linda Rumgay, Merle Sanders, Anne and Eleanor Sather, Betty Sheedy, Thurston Skei, Howard Slonecker, Britt Smith, Cecil and Molly Smith, E. White Smith, Lucie Sorensen-Smith, Herb and Betty Spady, Bill Stipe, Fran Summner, Ray Talbot, Victoria Tanner, Willard and Margaret Thompson, Carl Tuomala, H. Vaartnou, Cy Ward, Elsie Watson, Lynn Watts, Evelyn Weejes, Catherine Weeks, Milton Wildfong, Walter Wilkes, Arthur Wright, Jr., Rollin G. Wryens.

INTRODUCTION

When Captain George Vancouver's surgeon-botanist Archibald Menzies disembarked the ship *Discovery* in 1792 and documented his finding of *Rhododendron macrophyllum* at the edge of Puget Sound, he stepped into a region that would one day become a hotbed of horticultural activity centered round the genus of his new-found shrub. One by one, this and subsequent events brought plant people and rhododendrons to converge on the Pacific West Coast, producing one of the most creative milieus in the world for the introduction and development of the rhododendron as "king of shrubs."

The story of this convergence of plants and people on the West Coast is a story of both extraordinary plants and extraordinary people. The genus *Rhododendron* exhibits a richness of form, foliage, and flower beyond compare. From magnificent trees to sturdy shrubs to delicate groundcovers, rhododendrons play innumerable roles in the garden by their form alone. Foliage textures run the gamut from enormous, tropical-like leaves to exquisitely whorled collars of deep green leaves to minuscule jewel-like leaves. Add to this the range of flower color that offers seemingly infinite choices of hue, shade and tint, and the result is a genus that can excite the imagination of the most complacent horticulturist. But this is only half the story. The other half is the people who were so captivated by the genus they devoted their lives to its introduction into the garden and its improvement through hybridization. They are men and women with a mission. Though varying in style, temperament, and background, they seek each other out, bound by their shared enthusiasm. In their communications with each other whether by letter or person-to person, they learn, instruct, entertain, amuse, amaze, frustrate, madden, and even play jokes on each other. However, to a person, they share a public spiritedness, a willingness to share with each other and with the gardening public the fruits of their labors. This spirit of generosity eventually gave birth to the American Rhododendron Society, which facilitated communication on the genus worldwide.

After Archibald Menzies sent his Puget Sound specimen of *Rhododendron macrophyllum* to Kew Gardens in England for classification some 200 years ago, the story of the rhododendron on the West Coast moves at first in fits and starts. The next key events, in fact, occurred on the other side of the globe where plant explorers were finding new species in the mountains of western China and the Himalaya and sending seed home to Britain. But once the word was out on the splendor of these plants, here and there people on the West Coast were drawn in, and once they saw for themselves the desirability of rhododendrons for the maritime West Coast climate, there was no stopping them.

CHAPTER 1

THE BEGINNINGS

THE WEST COAST NATIVES

In the world of rhododendrons, the strong tie between Britain and the Pacific West Coast existed from the start. On May 4, 1792, when Archibald Menzies first laid eyes on *Rhododendron macrophyllum* in Puget Sound, he was collecting plants for his king's garden, King George III of England, not for the new American President George Washington or for any other North American dignitary. Menzies had been sent from England by Sir Joseph Banks of Kew Gardens to explore the Pacific Northwest with Captain George Vancouver and collect plants. Menzies, surgeon-botanist for the expedition, represents the long and passionate involvement by the British in botany and plant exploration. The early North American rhododendron growers would come to rely heavily on the British for their vast knowledge of plants and the botanical institutions they founded.

The Linnean Society of London

Archibald Menzies

The 1792 expedition headed by Captain George Vancouver with the two ships *Discovery* and *Chatham* covered the shoreline areas bounded on the south by Puget Sound and the current sites of Tacoma and Olympia, Washington, into Hood Canal, to Whidbey, Camano and San Juan Islands, up the Strait of Georgia between Vancouver Island and what is now British Columbia mainland, and north to Johnstone Strait. Banks instructed Menzies to collect dried specimens, seeds, and living plants so that "their names and qualities can be ascertained at His Majesty's gardens at Kew" (Justice 1991). The living plants were to be kept in "hutches," which proved to be highly unreliable during storms at sea.

When Menzies first saw *Rhododendron macrophyllum* at Discovery Bay in Puget Sound in May of 1792, it was not in bloom, but in June after a sighting of the rhododendron either on Bainbridge Island or Whidbey Island, a journal entry reads: "We also met here pretty frequent in the wood with that beautiful native of the Levant the purple rhododendron" (Justice 1991). Menzies called it *R. ponticum*, thinking it the same species as the *R. ponticum* native to the Caucasus Mountains of Europe. The name "macrophyllum" was later ascribed by British botanist David Don.

While the early settlers of the West Coast were most certainly unaware of the botanizing of *Rhododendron macrophyllum* by the British, they were captivated by the lovely shrub with its violet flowers and brought it into their gardens, sometimes mistakenly calling it a laurel.

The delicately flowered, fragrant West Coast native azalea *Rhododendron occidentale* was discovered by the English expedition headed by Captain Beechey in 1827. Seed was sent to Veitch Nurseries in England where it first flowered in 1857 and has since often been crossed with the Ghent, Knap Hill, and Exbury hybrid azaleas. The name of this lovely species, distributed along the coast from California to Oregon along streams and in open fields, has changed in response to botanists' attempts at classification, first referred to as *Azalea calendulacea*, then *A. californica*, and then *A. occidentalis*. In 1876, the American botanist Asa Gray placed it in the genus *Rhododendron*, and it was given its current name *R. occidentale*. Other early-recorded collections were made by James Barto in 1930 near Junction City, Oregon; by Leonard Frisbie in 1954 at Sugar Loaf Mountain, Oregon; and by Marie Kelly in 1959 in Mendocino County, California.

Five other rhododendrons are native to the Pacific West Coast, although their use in the garden and in hybridizing has been limited. The yellow flowering azalea *Rhododendron albiflorum* prefers mountain sites near the tree-line and is difficult in cultivation at lower elevations. The low-growing *Rhododendron camtschaticum* of southern Alaska is amenable to cultivation and a popular rock garden plant. *Rhododendron groenlandicum*, *R. neoglandulosum*, and *R. tomentosum* ssp. *subarcticum*, all moved from genus *Ledum* to *Rhododendron* in 1990, are native to northern regions of the West Coast.

Theories of the distribution of the genus *Rhododendron*, whose native habitats today circle the globe, are of interest to many rhododendron aficionados. They ask both why the distribution is so widespread—on all continents except South America, Africa, and Antarctica—and why the concentration is greater in some areas, such as the Himalayas and western China, and less in others, such as the Pacific West Coast.

The current and most accepted theory today, proposed by E. Irving and R. Hebda and discussed in the *Journal American Rhododendron Society* in 1993, is that rhododendrons were more widely and continuously distributed across North America and Eurasia during the milder climate some 65 million years ago during the Tertiary geologic era. Before the onset of the glacial periods, rhododendrons during their early history could have extended more or less continuously from North America to Greenland and Europe and eastward into China and northeastern Asia. During this time the "region of extreme relief" in the Tibet-Himalayan region, characterized by steep-sided mountain and deep valleys, did not even exist. However, as the climate changed and conditions became hostile with the development of glaciers, grasslands and deserts, rhododendron populations became isolated in those regions where they could survive. The collision of India with Asia, starting about 40 million years ago as a result of continental drift, created a region favorable to rhododendrons—the region of extreme relief. Today this region is home to the great bulk of rhododendrons we grow in our gardens today. The theory is that with the onset of the hostile environment, populations of rhododendrons at the margins of this area were able to enter the region of extreme relief and take advantage of newly developing and more amenable conditions. From here, the theory goes, the vireyas spread into the high-island archipelago in the Indo-Malaysian region.

THE INTRODUCTION OF EXOTIC SPECIES

Although the Pacific West Coast of North America offered its inhabitants several fine native rhododendrons for their gardens, the region of extreme relief in the Himalayas and western China proved to be the mother lode for spectacular discoveries of new rhododendron species that would find their way to the West Coast.

These new rhododendron discoveries in the nineteenth and early twentieth centuries were primarily made by the British, who once again proved to be a vital link in the cultivation of rhododendrons on the West Coast. The new American devotees loved the species for themselves, but they also used them as parents and began to create their own dynasty of Pacific West Coast hybrids.

One of the earliest introductions was *Rhododendron arboreum* from the region of extreme relief in India. H. H. Davidian, in *Rhododendron Species Volume II, Part I*, ascribes its introduction in 1810 to Scotsman Francis Buchanan-Hamilton who sent seed to Britain. This tree species bearing blood-red flowers not only made its way to the relatively mild climate of northern California but contributed to the lineage of some of the truly great West Coast hybrids: 'Trude Webster', 'Lem's Cameo', 'Anna Rose Whitney', 'Noyo Brave', 'Point Defiance', 'One Thousand Butterflies' and 'Bambino'.

In 1850 Sir Joseph Dalton Hooker introduced to Britain an astounding forty-five new rhododendron species from Sikkim, changing forever the role of the rhododendron in the garden, in both Britain and North America. Again, the species were admired and collected by West Coast growers, but, in addition, the great influx of new genes magnified the rhododendron hybridizing possibilities and inspired nurserymen and amateur gardeners alike to breed species with species and dream. Hooker's introduction *Rhododendron campylocarpum* contributed to the parentage of West Coast hybrids 'Golden Pheasant' and 'Odee Wright', which also bear yellow flowers. Hooker's introductions *R. maddenii* and *R. dalhousiae*, both of subsection *Maddenia*, have played a part in the development of tender, fragrant hybrids suitable for California gardens or patios further north where they can be protected during freezing weather.

The species introduced by Hooker that most influenced West Coast hybrids, however, is *Rhododendron griffithianum*, growing to the stature of a small tree with flaking bark and bearing large, white, saucer-shaped fragrant flowers. It plays a part in the lineage of 'Trude Webster', 'Lem's Cameo', 'Anna Rose Whitney', 'Hallelujah', 'Old Copper', 'Point Defiance', 'Naselle', 'Starbright Champagne', and 'One Thousand Butterflies'.

Another species of great influence among West Coast hybrids is *Rhododendron fortunei*, introduced in 1856 by Robert Fortune who discovered it in eastern China. Its fragrant, pale pink flowers and its reddish petioles are characteristic of the species, but its cold hardiness and heat tolerance make it especially useful in hybridizing. *Rhododendron fortunei* contributes to the parentage of West Coast hybrids 'Autumn Gold', 'Endre Ostbo', 'Hallelujah', 'Kimberly', 'King of Shrubs', 'Odee Wright', Olympic Lady Group, 'Horizon Monarch', 'Nancy Evans', 'Hotei', 'Ring of Fire', 'September Song', 'Senator Henry Jackson', 'Midnight Mystique', and 'Paprika Spiced'.

Two species discovered by the French missionary-explorer the Rev. Jean Soulié were *Rhododendron souliei* in 1893 and the closely related *R. wardii* in 1895; Frank Kingdon-Ward

discovered *R. wardii* again in 1913 and the plant was named for him. With its orbicular leaves and saucer-shaped pink or white flowers, *R. souliei* is an attractive species and has lent its influence in the parentage of 'Endre Ostbo', 'Horizon Monarch', 'Nancy Evans', 'Hotei', 'Top Banana', 'Butter Brickle', and 'Paprika Spiced'.

Rhododendron wardii, also with saucer-shaped flowers but yellow in hue, has contributed to West Coast hybrids 'Goldbug', 'Virginia Richards', 'Horizon Monarch', 'Nancy Evans', 'Top Banana', 'Ring of Fire', 'Bob Bovee', 'Butter Brickle', 'Orange Marmalade', and 'Coral Mist'.

George Forrest discovered the orange flowered *Rhododendron dichroanthum* in 1906 in Yunnan, China. This spreading and densely foliaged rhododendron, bearing its orange flowers in a lax truss and exhibiting a fawn indumentum on the undersides of its dark green leaves, would play an important part in the lineage of many West Coast hybrids, including 'Lem's Cameo', 'Autumn Gold', 'King of Shrubs', 'Kubla Khan', 'Old Copper', 'Thor', 'Horizon Monarch', 'Naselle', 'Hotei', Nancy Evans', 'Top Banana', 'Ring of Fire', 'September Song', 'Tahitian Dawn', 'Bambino', 'Starbright Champagne', 'Butter Brickle', 'Midnight Mystique', 'Coral Mist', 'Paprika Spiced', and 'One Thousand Butterflies'.

Greer

Rhododendron wardii

Greer

Rhododendron dichroanthum

The introduction of *Rhododendron williamsianum* by E. H. Wilson in 1908 from western China added an important species to the pool of rhododendrons from which West Coast hybridizers would draw to create their new beauties. The compact, dome-shaped shrub with heart-shaped leaves and nodding pink flowers would contribute its genes to 'Hallelujah', 'Kimberly', 'Lori Eichelser', Olympic Lady Group.

One of the most influential of the new species to come out of the Himalaya-Western China region was *Rhododendron griersonianum*, discovered by George Forrest in 1917. With lance-shaped leaves in matte green with white indumentum on the undersides and bright red flowers, this species has contributed its genes to innumerable West Coast hybrids: 'Anna Rose Whitney', 'Autumn Gold', 'Etta Burrows', 'Golden Pheasant', 'King of Shrubs', 'Old Copper', 'Virginia Richards', 'Vulcan's Flame', 'Naselle', 'Ring of Fire', 'September Song', 'Yaku Sunrise', 'Tahitian Dawn', 'Starbright Champagne', 'Cupcake', and 'Midnight Mystique'.

Two species from Japan would also contribute mightily to West Coast hybridizers' growing gene pool. The lepidote *Rhododendron keiskei* was introduced in 1908. This yellow-flowered shrub, varying in form from upright to prostrate, would play a significant role in producing small shrubs

useful in many landscape features. Among the West Coast hybrids with *R. keiskei* in their parentage are "Patty Bee', 'Ginny Gee', 'Shamrock', and 'Honsu's Baby'.

The elegant species *Rhododendron degronianum* ssp. *yakushimanum* (formerly classified as *R. yakushimanum*) reached Britain in 1934 when Lionel de Rothschild received two plants from a nursery in Japan. Although this mounding species with silver indumentum on its recurved leaves and with delicate pink flowers is hard to surpass, hybridizers have used it repeatedly in their crosses, creating 'Noyo Brave', 'Senator Henry Jackson', 'Cinnamon Bear', 'Golfer', 'Skookumchuck', 'Bambino', 'Bob Bovee', 'Cupcake', 'Mavis Davis', and 'Orange Marmalade'.

The discovery of the fragrant, tender species of subsection *Maddenia* added further possibilities for hybridizing, especially in California. *Rhododendron johnstoneanum*, introduced by Frank Kingdon-Ward in 1927 from Assam, bears fragrant flowers in colors from white to pink to yellow and contributes to the lineage of 'Rose Scott', with flowers of pink and a tinge of yellow. Joseph Dalton Hooker discovered the fragrant *R. lindleyi* in 1849 in Sikkim, and T. J. Booth discovered *R. nuttallii*, with its attractive new red growth, wrinkled mature foliage, and fragrant white flowers, in Assam in the same year. A

Greer

Rhododendron williamsianum

Greer

Rhododendron griersonianum

primary cross of these species produced the outstanding 'Mi Amor' that bears fragrant, white bell-shaped flowers up to 6 inches wide.

A species that recently has become popular with West Coast hybridizers is *Rhododendron proteoides*, discovered by George Forrest in his 1912-1914 China expedition and reintroduced by Joseph Rock in 1949.

East Coast native rhododendrons also have contributed to the hybridizing efforts on the West Coast. The hardy *Rhododendron catawbiense* was introduced in Britain in 1809 and found its way to the West Coast for use in hybridizing, mainly for its hardiness. Among West Coast hybrids carrying its genes are 'Trude Webster', 'Lem's Monarch', 'Odee Wright', 'Virginia Richards', 'Red Walloper', 'Point Defiance', 'Horizon Monarch', 'Skookumchuck', and 'Very Berry'.

The deciduous azalea *Rhododendron molle* was introduced to Britain from China in 1823 and was used in the development of the Exbury azaleas, a group that the West Coast hybridizers Ivan and Robertha Arneson of Oregon used extensively in their crosses.

The introduction of the evergreen azalea to the West Coast came primarily through the introduction of hybrid groups: the Southern Indian hybrids from southeastern United States and the Kurume and Satsuki hybrids from Ja-

pan, all of which were used by Nuccio's Nursery in Altadena, California, in its hybridizing program.

The introduction of the tender vireya rhododendrons from Southeast Asia, western Malaysia, and New Guinea was begun by the Veitch Nursery at approximately the same time Joseph Dalton Hooker discovered forty-five new rhododendron species in the Himalayas. *Rhododendron jasminiflorum*, *R. javanicum*, and *R. brookeanum* were among the species the Veitch Nursery used in their hybridizing. In 1961, Hermann Sleumer of the Netherlands published a description of nearly 100 vireya rhododendrons in *Flora Malesiana*, some of them previously discovered and some his own discoveries, including *R. aurigeranum*, with its spectacular yellow flowers in full trusses. West Coast vireya hybridizers would realize the suitability of these rhododendrons for the California climate and produce their own hybrids, one of which is 'Avalon' with *R. aurigeranum* as a parent.

THE INTRODUCTION OF EUROPEAN HYBRIDS

The newly discovered rhododendron species from Asia gradually made their way to North America, mostly through British channels, but at the same time the British were busily crossing the new species of Asia and North America to create their own hybrids, aiming for hardy plants that would grow in their climate. At first the emphasis was on crossing one hardy species with another using *Rhododendron campanulatum*, *R. barbatum*, *R. maximum*, and *R. catawbiense* and others, producing the supremely hardy

Greer

Rhododendron johnstoneanum

'Everestianum', 'Album Elegans', and 'Roseum Elegans. *Rhododendron* 'Cunningham's White', a hardy white, owes its parentage to *R. caucasicum* and *R. ponticum*. However, once *R. arboreum* arrived from Sikkim, this less hardy plant was crossed with a hardy cross of *R. catawbiense* with *R. ponticum* to produce 'Altaclerense' with dark red flowers. *Rhododendron* 'Nobleanum' was achieved by a cross of *R. caucasicum* with *R. arboreum*.

When *Rhododendron griffithianum* arrived, this species was put to use by the British to produce such noteworthy plants as 'Beauty of Littleworth' and 'Loder's White'. Both *R. griffithianum* and *R. fortunei* contribute to the parentage of the voluptuous Loderi Group, so important as parents for many West Coast hybrids. The most famous of the hardy hybrids, 'Pink Pearl', contains both *R. griffithianum* and *R. arboreum* in its genes along with the hardy East Coast native *R. catawbiense* and was first exhibited in Britain in 1896.

The so-called ironclad rhododendrons, a list of which was published in 1917 by E. H. Wilson of the Arnold Arboretum, Jamaica Plain, Massachusetts, included fourteen cultivars most of which were imported to North America from the Waterer Nursery in England. Among them were 'Album Elegans', 'Album Grandiflorum', 'Catawbiense Album', 'Everestianum', 'Purpureum Elegans', and 'Roseum Elegans'.

Before World War I when the glasshouse was in wide use in Britain, the tender Asian species contributed to a number of fragrant hybrids including 'Countess of Haddington' (*R. ciliatum* x *R. dalhousiae*), 'Lady Alice Fitzwilliam' (*R. edgeworthia* x *R. ciliatum*?), and 'Fragrantissimum' (*R. edgeworthii* x *R. formosum*). These crosses were later of great interest to West Coast hybridizers in California.

The British hybrids of the nineteenth century contributed significantly to the West Coast hybridizing efforts along with the species.

THE BENIGN WEST COAST CLIMATE

While North American East Coast hybridizers were focusing on rhododendrons hardy enough for the freezing temperatures of its rigorous winters, West Coast growers and hybridizers were discovering, to their delight, that the West Coast climate was amenable to a much wider range of rhododendrons. The USDA Plant Hardiness Zone Map shows the contrast between the East Coast and West Coast. The coastal areas of the Northeast range from Zone 5a to 7b. This represents a spread of average minimum temperatures from -20°F (-29°C) to 5°F (-15°C), all of which are well below freezing, of course. In the coastal areas of the Southeast, excluding Florida, zones range from Zone 7b to 8b, representing a spread of average minimum temperatures from 5°F (-15°C) to 15°F (-9°C), again, well below freezing. Florida, on the other hand, contains regions where, on the average, no freezing temperatures occur.

The USDA Plant Hardiness Zone Map presents a different picture of the North American West Coast. The coldest coastal zone is Zone 8a and the warmest is Zone 10b, representing a spread of average minimum temperatures from 10°F (-12°C) to 35°F (2°C). In the world of rhododendrons, there is a great difference between a low of -20°F, the East Coast lowest average minimum, and 10°F, the West Coast lowest average minimum.

In British Columbia in the north, the immediate coastal areas fall within Zone 8b (20°F to 15°F; -7°C to -10°C), although within 10 miles of the coastline, the zone can drop to 8a (15°F to 10°F; -10°C to -12°C). Patches of Zone 9a (25°F to 20°F; -4°C to -7°C) occur, especially on the west coast of Vancouver Island.

In Washington, the narrow coastal area bordering Puget Sound falls in Zone 8b, with the rest of western Washington up to the foothills of the Cascade Mountains in Zone 8a. A patch of Zone 9a occurs on the northeast corner of the Olympic Peninsula.

A wide strip of Zone 8b occurs in western Oregon backed by Zone 8a to the east. However, on the Oregon Coast narrow patches of Zone 9a occur, and a large patch of Zone 9b (30°F to 25°F; -1°C to -4°C) occurs in the southwest.

In the coastal areas of California, Zone 8b virtually disappears, giving way to the warmer Zone 9b and Zone 10a (35°F to 30°F; 2°C to -1°C). Zone 9b, with average minimum low temperature a few degrees below freezing, predominates in northern California to San Francisco, with patches of Zone 10a (35°F to 30°F; 2°C to -1°C) in Humboldt County and San Francisco.

In southern California coastal areas, Zone 10a predominates with spots of Zone 10b (40°F to 35°F; 4°C to 2°C) at Santa Barbara and further south.

Hawaii falls almost entirely in Zone 11 (40°F and above; 5°C and above).

A map of hardiness zones will, of course, fail to tell the whole climate story—or even the whole temperature range story. The average minimum *high* temperatures, microclimates, the timing of a season's first freeze, and numerous other factors affect rhododendron hardiness. Nevertheless, the USDA zones, first of all, make clear the West Coast is milder than the East Coast and, second of all, illustrate in detail the range of temperature zones that do exist on the West Coast, affecting the choice of rhododendron varieties that will grow well in a particular area. The goals of hybridizers will also be affected by climate in which they live, for they usually try to produce plants that will do well in their own area. Choosing plants that do well in a particular area, and producing even better plants for that area continues to be a goal of rhododendron hobbyists and professionals alike.

Temperature, of course, is only one factor contributing to climate. Rainfall is another major factor, especially when it comes to the moisture-loving genus *Rhododendron*. Generally, rainfall on the West Coast is greater in the north, diminishing to the south. Indicating this trend is the average annual rainfall for the major cities: Vancouver, British Columbia, 60 inches; Seattle, 33 inches; Portland, 37 inches; San Francisco, 21 inches; Los Angeles, 15 inches. However, much variation occurs within each area because of the varying topography. In all regions, the bulk of the precipitation occurs from October to May, leaving the summer months both the driest and warmest. This characteristic has led horticulturists to term the climate "Mediterranean." Also during the wet season, cloud cover is common, and moisture-laden breezes off the ocean, even in summer, contribute moisture and reduce dehydration.

During the winter months, the mild temperatures, continual rainfall, moisture-laden maritime air bathing the coast, and cloud cover all are conducive to the growing of rhododendrons. During the summer months, however, irrigation is often necessary.

THE GREAT EXPOSITIONS

Once the great influx of Asian rhododendron species and hybrids from Britain became available on the West Coast, gardeners and professional horticulturists soon realized how fortunate they were to live in such a rhododendron-friendly climate. Then, in the early 1900s, two public events occurred which fueled the fire of enthusiasm over rhododendrons even

Lewis & Clark Exposition

more. In a centennial celebration of the Lewis and Clark expedition, Portland, Oregon, hosted the first world's fair west of the Rocky Mountains in June 1905 to commemorate the expedition and to advertise to the world the climate, geography, and industry of Oregon. Swiss nurseryman John G. Bacher, who would become instrumental in developing interest in rhododendrons on the West Coast and become a founding member of the Portland Chapter of the American Rhododendron Society, visited the fair. He was so impressed with the exposition site and its views of snow-capped mountain peaks breaking a horizon

of rolling blue and green that he decided to make Portland his home. Bacher said, "It was not long till I knew I would never go back to Europe, not to stay, that is. I realized I could never return to the narrower dimensions of life in my native land" (Poole 1988). Stay, he did and contributed mightily to the momentum of the West Coast's enthrallment with the genus *Rhododendron*.

In 1915, San Francisco hosted the Panama-Pacific Exposition to which Japanese nurseryman Kokiro Akashi of Kurume on the island of Kyushu sent an exhibit of thirty Kurume evergreen azaleas. Up to this time, the evergreen azaleas were almost unknown in western United States. Toichi Domoto, a nurseryman from Hayward, California, recalls that his father, after seeing the azaleas at the Panama-Pacific Exposition, traveled to Japan to meet the growers of the Kurume azaleas and government officials of Kurume. As a result, the growers and the officials gave the Domotos the exclusive sales rights to the Kurume azaleas in the United States. West Coast nurserymen were delighted to have this new evergreen azalea and saw its popularity as a landscape plant flourish. In 1918 Ernest Henry Wilson also visited Kurume and at the Akashi Nursery selected fifty cultivars to send to the Arnold Arboretum. These became known as "Wilson's Fifty." West Coast hybridizers, including Nuccio's Nursery of Altadena, California, Bill Guttormsen of Canby, Oregon, the Sherwood Nursery of Corbett, Oregon, and Garda Griswold of Kirkland, Washington, would use the Kurume azaleas to produce their own hybrids suitable for their climate.

Golden Gate Park Superintendent John McLaren landscaped the fair and was determined to have the finest show of rhododendrons ever seen in America. He ordered the best rhododendrons from Belgium, Holland, and England, including 'Cornubia', 'Loderi', and 'Cynthia'. After the exposition, the plants were moved to a dell in Golden Gate Park.

One event after another moved the genus *Rhododendron* into the forefront of horticultural activity on the West Coast until a series of governmental actions severely impeded the importation of nursery stock. A series of quarantines, culminating with Plant Quarantine No. 37 in 1919, severely curtailed the importation of all plant material from Britain and Europe to the United States, and from Oregon to other states. West Coast nurserymen were forced to set a new course to satisfy the growing demand for rhododendrons, devising new and ingenious methods of propagation.

CHAPTER 2

THE PIONEERS

IN OREGON

John G. Bacher, the Swiss nurseryman who was so impressed by the 1905 Lewis and Clark centennial celebration he moved to Portland the next year, was well equipped to deal with the crisis the quarantines had imposed on the nursery industry. This small, bespectacled man, so trim in bearing he personified the precision and orderliness for which his nursery would become known, became a pioneer rhododendron propagator in his new West Coast home.

John Bacher had graduated second in his class from the National School of Horticulture of Geneva in 1900 at the age of 18 years and easily secured jobs in horticulture in Europe after his graduation. Bacher, however, was also a restless adventurer and sought new opportunities in America. In 1902, in Grand Rapids, Michigan, he planted the state's first cherry orchard. From there he moved to St. Louis,

Van Veen

John Bacher

Missouri, where he continued his interest in cherries for another four years. In 1906, after visiting the Lewis and Clark centennial site, he made his final move to a new country resembling his mountainous homeland in Switzerland. Here he would stay until his death in 1961.

At age 24, after establishing a home in Portland with his wife, Louise, Bacher's first entrepreneurial venture was to found the Swiss Floral Company at 1920 Northeast 7th Ave., Portland. Although Bacher knew that the best chance for financial success came through specializing in one group of plants, his boundless interest in all plants led to a business that encompassed bulbs, succulents, tropicals, petunias and, eventually, rhododendrons. His success is largely attributed to his meticulous attention to "consistent maintenance of basic practices" (Poole 1988). This involved a rigorous and methodical attention to plants. Proof of this practice are in Bacher's journals which include entries on temperature, bloom time, and arrival of bulb shipments from Holland. The repetitive but essential ingredients of plant maintenance, involving record upon record of details, Bacher considered basic to horticultural success. At this he was a master.

Also essential to his business was propagation of seed obtained through international sources in order to satisfy the gardening public's demand for exotic plants. Known as a "propagation wizard," Bacher inevitably ventured into the propagation of Asian rhododendrons to satisfy gardeners' thirst for these valuable landscape plants. When Joseph Rock made his expedition to China in 1932, Bacher obtained 375 packets of seeds and grew the plants on to blooming size—sometimes as long as ten years. Now captivated by the genus, Bacher himself contributed financially and helped raise funds for an expedition by Frank Kingdon-Ward to Burma in 1948 to collect rhododendron seed.

Bacher felt that gardening was a democratic activity for all levels of society. He created a momentum among professionals and amateurs to find and grow the best of the genus for all to enjoy. By the time enough rhododendrons and rhododendron lovers had converged in the Portland area to form an organized horticultural group, John Bacher was ready to lead. It was his philosophy that would form the heart of the American Rhododendron Society

Another European trained nurseryman was to affect profoundly the gardening public's enchantment with rhododendrons on the West Coast. Theodore Van Veen, Sr., born in 1881 near Arnhem, Holland, was trained in a country with a long tradition of horticultural excellence. Even the name Van Veen means "of the soil." Like Bacher, Van Veen emigrated to North America to use his horticultural skills in his new home. In 1906, Van Veen arrived in British Columbia to earn his livelihood as a horticulturist. He moved to Seattle in 1915 and then to Durham, Oregon, a suburb of Portland, to work for the J. B. Pilkington Nursery. Then, while working as a gardener for prominent Portland banker Elliot Corbett, he began his own backyard nursery.

In 1926 Theodore Van Veen, Sr., established the Van Veen Nursery at its present location at 4201 S. E. Franklin St., Portland. Using horses to plow and harrow the one-acre lot, previously used to grow pansies, Van Veen's first offerings of rhododendrons were azaleas, among them 'Altaclarensis', 'J. C. van Tol', 'Hinode Giri', and various species. The azaleas were started by seed in cold frames covered with a glass sash 3 by 6 feet (1 by 2 m) with a plaster lath frame for shade. Several times each day the glass, together with the lath, had to be raised for hand watering. A roll of muslin cloth lay at the end of each cold frame for covering when the sun became too intense. If warm weather persisted, a small block was placed under each end for an opening to reduce the high temperature. German peatmoss, shipped in large, compressed bales bound with baling wire stapled to pieces of lath running the length of the bale, served as a propagating medium. The peat was chipped off with a pitchfork and pounded into usable form—a hot, dusty, and tedious task.

Van Veen was determined to propagate rhododendrons from cuttings, a little known technique in the 1920s. The best time to take cuttings, the proper method of trimming, satisfactory rooting media, and water requirements all had to be learned by trial. After the quarantine, however, rhododendron propagation was essential if the public was going to acquire this great genus.

A break came with the availability of cheap electrical power from the new Bonneville dam. Oregon State University was seeking new uses for electricity in horticulture and, as a result, a heating cable was developed, which Van Veen tried

in one of the cold frames to create a kind of sweatbox. At first it proved unreliable for lack of a moisture-proof thermostat. Yet, by 1932, Van Veen's success rate of cuttings was 78 percent, which was excellent for the time. Hormones did not exist, but Van Veen experimented with various sugar dips, including honey, molasses, and potassium permanganate. Since named hybrids were generally unavailable, he collected cuttings from friends, parks, and cemeteries. These early propagations were unnamed and listed by flower description, such as "pink edge, ashy-pink center."

About 1934 Van Veen constructed a Dutch greenhouse, consisting of a deep trench wide enough for a walkway down the center and length, with propagation benches at ground level on each side. An A-frame of two-by-fours supported the glass sash used on the cold frames, set lengthwise from soil line to peak. Another set of glass cov-

Van Veen

Theodore Van Veen, Sr. and his cold frames

Van Veen

Van Veen's First Dutch Greenhouse

ered the beds to increase humidity. Newspapers were placed over the glass to keep out hot sun. Then, in 1940, he successfully developed a misting system for propagation with the help of a heating engineer friend who used oil burner nozzles for the mist spray, setting a pattern for propagation throughout the world.

Records at the Van Veen Nursery show that as early as the 1930s Van Veen was communicating with rhododendron growers Joseph Gable of Stewartstown, Pennsylvania, and James Barto of Junction City, Oregon, and exchanging ideas and plant material. During the early 1930s, the nursery received a shipment of budded stock rhododendrons from Cottage Gardens Nursery in Eureka, California. The plants came up the coast

by boat, packed with excelsior in coffin-like boxes. Among the plants was *Rhododendron* 'Pink Pearl', a cross by John Waterer and the most famous hardy English hybrid, first exhibited in 1896. 'Pink Pearl' was used to produce hundreds of plants for West Coast gardeners.

Theodore Van Veen, Sr., involved his son, Ted Van Veen, in the work of the nursery from the time he was a young boy through his teenage years. Ted recalls his father's pride in keeping the nursery in "Dutch-clean" order. When Ted was a teenager during the Depression, he replaced the horses and hand-spaded the fields. "Experience taught me to turn the soil to a reasonable good depth, and at the same time with minimum effort reduce the clods to a small size, all the while maintaining an even soil level" (Ted Van Veen 1982). When he was old enough to use a three-pronged push cultivator, he "plodded up and down each row, stripped to the waist. The flying dust covered my upper torso and streamed up my pant legs" (Ted Van Veen 1982). A scuffle hoe, with a long handle enabling a wide reach from one position and with a single, 5-inch-long half-moon blade sharpened on both sides, was also used for weeding. To conserve moisture in the soil during Portland's hot summers, a Dutch technique of lightly hand cultivating the top crust of soil after a rainfall or watering and then shuffling by foot along the rows reduced the soil to a fine dust, creating a mulch to slow evaporation.

After the Depression, Theodore Van Veen further developed his nursery into a successful business. He established a reputation as a rhododendron grower and hybridizer and maintained his enthusiasm until the day he died in 1961 at age 80. Among his crosses using (*R. fortunei* ssp. *discolor* x Fabia Group) are 'Evening Glow', 'Autumn Gold', and 'Maryke', all products of his search for a good yellow. His hybrids 'Lucky Strike', 'Anna Rose Whitney' and 'Van' are results of the cross (*R. griersonianum* x 'Countess of Derby'). His hybrid 'Old Copper' is the result of the cross ('Vulcan' x Fabia Group), and 'Van Veen' the result of (*R. griersonianum* x 'Pygmalion').

Like Bacher, this skilled and public-spirited nurseryman was ready to support a rhododendron society when the time was right.

While John Bacher and Theodore Van Veen were building their nurseries in Portland, a carpenter moved his family from Chicago to homestead in the eastern foothills of Oregon's Coast Range ten miles west of Junction City. His name was James Barto. In the next twenty years, he would develop one of the finest rhododendron collections on the West Coast with some 500 species of which many forms were unsurpassed.

James Barto was born in Lewistown, Pennsylvania, in 1881. Though a sickly child, starting to school late, he was a keen student and quickly made up for lost time. After graduating from high school he trained as a carpenter, a trade he practiced all his life. In 1905 he enlisted in the U.S. Navy, and in 1913 he married Ruth Ellen Lampson. They made their home in Chicago, but

Van Veen

'Maryke'

Van Veen

James Barto

after the armistice, Barto heard that land in Oregon was open to homesteading for veterans and in 1920 headed west to investigate, filing for land near Junction City that would become the Barto home. He returned to Chicago, loaded his wife and children into an old truck and headed west.

For the remaining nineteen years of life, Barto continued to work at his trade during the week in Eugene and Corvallis, returning home to work all day Saturday and Sunday to make the Barto home more livable, to clear land, and to grow rhododendrons. Besides his extraordinary physical endurance, James Barto was endowed with unusual intellectual curiosity. He was an ardent reader and student. Once he became interested in a subject he pursued it exhaustively—chickens, rabbits, goats, minerals, and honey bees were explored in his pre-rhododendron days. He grew a variety of magnolias from imported seed, and tree peonies were imported from Japan, as were camellias, which proved unsatisfactory. He also grew *Davidia involucrata* (dove tree), *Gordonia*, *Cardiocrinum giganteum*, *Ilex* (holly) and *Delphinium*. His curiosity extended to Oregon native plants whose seeds he later sent to correspondents in exchange for rhododendron seeds.

Greer

Davidia involucrata (dove tree)

Barto's interest in rhododendrons began while employed by the firm Raup and York of Eugene to construct a greenhouse for growing potted azaleas for the florist trade. In 1925 he was given seed that he grew in a small flat on a chicken incubator heated by a kerosene lamp. His interest was peaked by these first seedlings, and he began to write letters to rhododendron growers in the United States, England, Scotland, Japan, and China. Mrs. A. C. U. Berry of Portland was extremely helpful and gave him more names of people with whom he could correspond and obtain seeds from plant collecting expeditions in Asia. Mrs. Chauncey Craddock of Eureka, California, an early rhododendron grower, also was of great help. He also corresponded with E. H. Wilson of the Arnold Arboretum, E. J. P. Magor of England, and the Royal Botanic Garden, Edinburgh, all of whom sent seeds. F. M. Ellis of Griffin, Georgia, sent seed of native eastern North American azaleas. Barto also received seed from Japanese nurseries and from Waterer & Sons & Crisp of England. He also corresponded and exchanged seed with Joseph Gable of Stewartstown, Pennsylvania.

Barto kept complete records of his rhododendrons, showing lists of collectors' numbers representing expeditions, and these numbers were written on paper tags sealed in small glass tubes in the lath house with the plants. Yet, because most of his correspondence and records were lost when fire destroyed the Barto home in 1940, sources of rhododendron seed Barto grew are largely unknown and can only be surmised, although some species he grew can be traced to certain expeditions, such as *Rhododendron decorum* with a small blotch, a form attributed to a discovery by Dr. Hu and Professor Yu, and other forms of *R. decorum* attributed E. H. Wilson, Frank Kingdon-Ward, and E. H. M. Cox. Barto's collection grew to cover the range of rhododendrons from the small subsection *Lapponica* to the big-leaf species to the azaleas.

The development of Barto's rhododendron collection on the homestead site required work beyond belief. However, two factors were in his favor: the favorable Northwest climate and virgin forest soil that was porous, high in humus, and well drained at its hillside location.

In 1926 the first greenhouse was built with heat provided by a wood stove with pipes circulating warm water under the beds. Soon it was filled with flats of small seedlings carefully labeled and recorded, spreading over the benches like a green lawn. Mrs. Barto said she would hear him talking to the little seedlings as if they were people. Then a lath house was built and filled with plants. Not knowing how much cold the small plants could tolerate, Barto enlisted his children to sack up maple leaves to cover the plants for winter.

Once the plants were large enough to move from the lath house, ground had to be cleared. With no machinery for the purpose, trees were hand felled and cut into wood for building materials. Huge stumps were blasted and pulled out by the horse, Shorty, for burning. Eventually five acres were cleared and planted with rhododendrons. Irrigation was needed during the dry summer months, and Barto secured water rights to a spring on adjacent land. A dam provided a water reservoir, and from it 2,700 feet (810 m) of pipe, with small holes bored in it, carried water to the plantings. (The family remembered that the length of the pipe corresponded to the number of miles they drove in the old truck from Chicago to Oregon.) Pressure on the line caused the water to shoot high into the air and scatter with the air currents, giving excellent distribution.

As more rhododendron seed arrived, a second greenhouse and lath house were needed. Without electricity or automatic control, wood fires provided heat that often needed refueling in the middle of the night.

Although James Barto provided momentum for the vast project, his family proved indispensable in its success. His wife, Ruth, and his six children, especially Pauline, Merrill and Donald, were actively involved in the work. Pauline recalls that "the constant weeding, watering, and transplanting were a never ending chore which involved the entire family" (Pauline Sandoz, personal communication). Each week before returning to work, Barto would lay out instructions for tasks that should be done while he was away.

An impelling fascination to collect, grow, and learn about rhododendrons was, apparently, James Barto's motivation. As a result of his letter writing he received visitors to whom he gave away thousands of plants, but James Barto never grew rhododendrons for commercial purposes.

In May 1940, Barto was admitted to the veterans' hospital in Portland for cancer and never returned home. In June of that year, the house burned down, destroying his library and records. Merrill was called into the military service so that all who remained on the homestead were Mrs. Barto, Pauline and young Donald. Maintenance of the collection proved an impossible task for the three Bartos, and plants were sold to visitors. Large and small rhododendrons were hauled away in truckloads. With the lack of knowledge of the species and the absence of the Barto records, some plants were used as understock for grafting with commercial hybrids, and others were dumped as garbage.

One of the visitors to the Barto homestead who salvaged several treasures was Dr. Carl Phetteplace. He visited the Barto home in 1944 and, among others, brought home a plant of

Greer

Rhododendron augustinii 'Blue Barto'

Rhododendron augustinii. The form was later named 'Barto Blue'—one of the best forms of this lovely species. Others who were fortunate to obtain Barto rhododendrons later recognized their worth. Among the named Barto species forms and hybrids are: 'Attar' (a form of *R. decorum*), 'Barto Alpine' (a subsection *Lapponica* hybrid), 'Barto Ivory' (probably a *R. fortunei* cross), 'Barto Lavender' (probably a *R. fortunei* and *R. ponticum* cross), 'Barto Rose' (a form of *R. oreodoxa* var. fargesii), 'Esquire' (a *R. griersonianum* cross), 'Fair Sky' (a form of *R. augustinii*), 'Finch' (a form of *R. rubiginosum* Desquamatum Group), 'James Barto' (probably a cross of *R. orbiculare* and *R. williamsianum*),

'Peachblow' (unknown parentage), 'Renaissance' ('Loderi King George' x Peter Koster'), 'Ruth Lyons' (form of *R. davidsonianum*), 'Spring Dance' (a *R. triflorum* cross), and 'Taiping' (unknown parentage).

Working in virtual isolation from other West Coast rhododendron growers, James Barto amassed a species collection that eventually was recognized for what it was: a supreme contribution to the growing of excellent species forms on the West Coast.

At the same time that Barto was building his rhododendron collection in the wilds near Junction City, Mrs. A. C. U. (Rae Selling) Berry, born in 1881, was building her garden in a stately residential area of Portland. Her botanical interests were wide-ranging—alpines, natives, and rhododendrons—and led her to create a garden that displayed her plants beautifully and naturalistically. Her interest in rhododendrons led her to support the botanical expeditions of Frank Kingdon-Ward and Joseph Rock, both of whom sent her seed. Results of her skillful propagation of seed from explorers and other sources are evident today in stands of tree-size *Rhododendron dis-*

Greer

Rhododendron fortunei

American Rhododendron Society Files

Mrs. A. C. U. (Rae Selling) Berry and Ray James

color and *R. calophytum*, two of 130 *Rhododendron* species in the garden. The splendid rock garden contains numerous alpine species, and the woodland is filled with rhododendrons, other exotic woodland dwellers, and native plants. In 1983, the Berry Botanic Garden began the Seed Bank for Rare and Endangered Plants of the Pacific Northwest and today is a member of the Center for Plant Conservation, a national network. The garden, now a private, non-profit organization, is open to the public.

Mrs. A. C. U. Berry is a charter member of the American Rhododendron Society and received its Gold Medal in 1962.

IN WASHINGTON

In the Puget Sound region, Reginald A. Pearce developed one of the earliest rhododendron nurseries in Kenmore, Washington. An Englishman who immigrated to the Pacific Northwest at the turn of the century, Pearce owned and operated the State Flower Nursery from 1920 to 1960. Pearce purchased the property soon after World War I and began collecting rare rhododendrons as well as making his own crosses. Among his hybrids still in the trade is 'Pearce's American Beauty' ('Mrs. C. S. Sargent' x 'Dr. H. C. Dresselhuys') with dark red flowers with green spotting. Many of his mature specimens and hybrids still grow in the Old Garden on the nursery site, which has been established by the King County Park System as the Kenmore Rhododendron Park and Garden. A new garden at the park was started in 1955 by Warren F. and Diane M. Timmons III, who now operate the park.

One of the earliest Washington rhododendron "ambassadors" was Donald G. Graham, Sr., of Seattle whose garden in the Broadmore section of the city eventually became home to some 500 varieties of rhododendrons. As early as the 1930s, Graham imported rhododendrons from Japan and England. During World War II, he was stationed with the 8th Air Force in England and visited Exbury, home of Edmund de Rothschild, and became well acquainted with this well-known grower and hybridizer. Graham was instrumental in the establishment of the University of Washington Arboretum (now the Washington Park Arboretum), which from its inception included selections of the genus *Rhododendron* in its woody plant collection. Graham's wife, Juanita, helped establish the volunteer group for the arboretum. In 1946, Donald Graham chaired the first rhododendron show, held in a tent in the arboretum, which 3,000 people attended. Both Donald and Juanita Graham were charter members of the American Rhododendron Society.

Greer

'Pearce's American Beauty'

IN CALIFORNIA

Several California nurseries contributed to the dawn of interest in rhododendrons in the southern West Coast region. Domoto's Nursery was the first distributor of the Kurume azaleas after their introduction to the California public at the Panama-Pacific Exposition in 1915 (see Chapter 1), but the nursery also carried the Belgian Indian azalea hybrids, Southern Indian azalea hybrids, and deciduous azaleas.

Coolidge Rare Plants Gardens of Pasadena introduced many varieties of the Kurume azaleas and the Mucronatum Group of azaleas that they developed from seed from Japan. Along with the azaleas they offered elepidote rhododendrons suitable for California: 'Pink Pearl', 'Mrs. G. W. Leak', and *Rhododendron ponticum*.

Kramer Bros. Nursery of Upland, California, was also an early proponent of rhododendrons, offering evergreen azaleas from the Kurume, Belgian Indian, and Southern Indian groups, along with the standard group of elepidotes adaptable for California. The Kramer brothers, Gus and Otto, were the first to introduce 'Anah Kruschke', a cross of 'Purple Splendour' with *Rhododendron ponticum* and still a popular plant in California. 'Anah Kruschke' was grown in Clackamas, Oregon by Franz Kruschke, a grower of florist azaleas, who named the plant after his wife, Anah Kruschke.

One of the most influential early California nurseries to introduce rhododendrons was Nuccio's in Altadena, California, which was begun in 1935 and still is a thriving business today. The founders, Joe and Julius Nuccio, started a backyard nursery in Alhambra while working the night shift at a glass factory. Their specialties were from the start azaleas and camellias as they are today.

Cottage Gardens Nursery on California's north coast at Eureka also pioneered the early efforts to grow and propagate rhododendrons. Its founder, Charles Willis Ward, a New York businessman suffering from "nervous prostration," was ordered by his physicians in 1888 to close his business and seek a quiet country life. As a result, he settled on Long Island, New York, where he began growing carnations as a hobby. His hobby evolved into a nursery business, Cottage Gardens, but failed to restore him to good health. In 1913, he was called to Eureka, California, regarding a legal dispute over redwood timbered lands of the David Ward estate of which he was part owner. He arrived in Humbolt County a sick man, but within ten days the climate began to restore his health, and in 1915 he moved to Eureka where he established Cottage Gardens Nursery nearby in Eden. On the 81-acre site at Eden, he built slat houses for thousands of evergreen azaleas and planted row upon row of rhododendrons and other shrubs and trees. Ward transported his plants to the Atlantic coast by rail in enormous quantity. Records show that in one year, the stock for sale included 50,000 azaleas and 50,000 rhododendrons. Ward became a millionaire, but by 1922 the nursery began having financial problems and he eventually went broke and the nursery fell into the hands of receivers. In 1985 the nursery was closed and the land sold to developers. During its operation Cottage Gardens Nursery supplied early, hardy English elepidote hybrids, such as 'Alice' and 'Pink Pearl', to the San Francisco Bay Area, southern California, and the Van Veen Nursery in Oregon.

The early pioneer California nurserymen, especially those in southern California, recognized the great landscape value of the evergreen azaleas in a warm coastal climate, and, as a result, the evergreen azalea was the first rhododendron to win the hearts of California gardeners.

But it was not long before Californians discovered many other rhododendrons would also thrive in the southern West Coast climates.

IN BRITISH COLUMBIA

Further north, in British Columbia, the beginnings of the rhododendron ground swell occurred earlier and in virtual isolation from the rest of the West Coast. George Fraser, born in 1854 in Scotland and trained in horticulture, immigrated to Manitoba, Canada, in 1883, and entered the greenhouse business. In 1894, twelve years before John Bacher moved to Portland,

Dale

George Fraser

Fraser had moved to Ucluelet, on the west coast of Vancouver Island, British Columbia, where he purchased 236 acres of native bush. Like John Bacher and Theodore Van Veen, Fraser came to his new home with skills learned in a country with a long tradition of horticultural professionalism. But, unlike the two Oregonians, he was isolated in the West Coast frontier. Access to the roadless region was by boat or crude logging trails over the mountains. To make connection with other rhododendron growers he reached out to Britain and the East Coast for people who shared his enthusiasms, including Joseph Gable and E. J. P. Magor.

Although restricted by isolation from other professional horticulturists, Fraser found the climate on the west coast of Vancouver Island, with its moist air from the Pacific Ocean and the warming influence of the Japanese Current, ideal for growing rhododendrons, including many tender varieties. Nevertheless, the labor involved in clearing the dense vegetation, improving the stony soil, and dealing with an annual rainfall of 120 inches (300 cm) was considerable. He built a system of underground drains of cedar planks and dressed the soil with seaweed and cow manure that he brought to the site on a small flat scow towed behind his rowboat. He constructed a rooting frame in a lean-to behind his house, providing bottom heat with a wood-burning heater. The heater was placed in a hole, and tiles carried the warm smoke underneath the rooting beds to the atmosphere on the other side.

As his nursery developed, tourists arrived by steamer to visit. Whether they bought plants or not, Fraser gave them a bouquet of flowers when they returned to the boat. However, Fraser conducted most of his business by mail. He sent plants to the Layritz Nursery in Victoria, carefully packed with sphagnum moss in wooden crates built of driftwood. By 1925, his catalog included azaleas, heaths, hollies, roses, pernettyas, rhododendrons and native hybrids. Fraser was much interested in the native plants of his new home, the native rose, honeysuckle, and gooseberry, which he crossed with domestic varieties to create superior plants.

From the start of his life in Ucluelet, Fraser was interested in rhododendrons. Yet his first and best-known rhododendron hybrid came by chance. In a shipment of cranberry sent from Nova Scotia in 1897, which he had intended to cross with the native variety, he found *Rhododendron canadense*, a wild azalea of eastern Canada and the United States. He planted it, and fifteen years later when it bloomed he crossed it with *R. molle* ssp. *japonicum*. In 1919 he sent a budded plant of the cross to the Arnold Arboretum, which failed to acknowledge it. He then sent a plant to Kew Gardens, where it was named 'Fraseri'. Independently, the Arnold Arboretum also named the plant 'Fraseri'. (The name was later changed to Fraseri Group.)

The same year, 1897, George Fraser began a life-long correspondence with Joseph Gable, who was put in touch with Fraser by E. H. Wilson. The letters from Fraser to Gable are now preserved in the Provincial Archives of British Columbia. They are a testament to the influence these two great rhododendron growers and hybridizers had on each other and document their

Van Veen

'Albert Close'

close friendship. Fraser was breaking new ground in the field of rhododendron hybridizing, testing his own theories relentlessly. He also discussed his theories with Gable by letter, for instance, his theory that sterile hybrids often become fertile with age. Fraser also introduced Gable to E. J. P. Magor by mail.

Joseph Gable, in a letter to Clive Justice of Vancouver, British Columbia, dated Nov. 8, 1960, wrote of his indebtedness to George Fraser: "So both I and those who grow and enjoy the varieties of rhododendrons I have concocted and disseminated owe a debt we can not figure in dollars and cents to the kindly paternal advice and generosity of my old friend George Fraser" (Dale 1990).

George Fraser, a bachelor, apparently was a great favorite in the community of Ucluelet. Children came to picnic, and Fraser would teach them about plants. He donated land on which the Ucluelet Athletic Club and two schools were built. His generosity extended to his friends afar. At Christmas he sent a box of holly and pernettya to Mrs. Gable and heather to friends in Winnipeg and Victoria.

George Fraser's named hybrids include: the Fraseri Group (*R. canadense* x *R. molle* ssp. *japonicum*; *R.* 'Albert Close' (*R. maximum* x 'Mrs. Jamie Fraser'); *R.* 'George Fraser' (*R. macrophyllum* x *R. maximum*); *R.* 'Maxie' (*R. maximum* x *R. macrophyllum*); *R.* 'Camich' (*R. catawbiense* x 'Michael Waterer'); the John Blair Group (*R. occidentale* x *R. arborescens*); and 'Mrs. Jamie Fraser' ([*R. arboreum* x *R. macrophyllum*] x *R. arboreum*). Bill Dale of Sidney, British Columbia, is building a collection of the Fraser hybrids at his home in Sidney.

Fraser's death in 1944 marked the end of his nursery. However, several rhododendrons he planted beside St. Columbus Church in Tofino on Vancouver Island in 1924 are now as high as the church. A George Fraser Memorial Garden has been planted in Ucluelet. In 1992, Fraser was honored at Christies Nursery in Scotland, where he had worked as a household servant and started his gardening career at age 17. A plaque was placed in recognition of the honor he had brought to his native land.

George Fraser died in his ninetieth year. He remained at his home in Ucluelet until his last days. When he was carried by his friends to a boat that would take him to the hospital in Port Alberni, Fraser said, "I don't know where I'm going to end up, but it doesn't matter. I have had my heaven on earth" (Dale 1990).

Almost forty years after George Fraser arrived in Ucluelet on the west coast of Vancouver Island, Ted and Mary Greig started their nursery at Royston in 1933 on the east coast of the island. Yet at this time, except for the old British and European hybrids, rhododendrons were still largely unknown among the gardening public. For the next thirty-three years, however, the Greigs developed a species rhododendron collection at their nursery that ignited the fires of rhododendron enthusiasm among British Columbia gardeners.

The Greig Nursery began when Ted and Mary bought the alpine nursery stock from George and Jeanne Buchanan Simpson at Cowichan Lake on Vancouver Island, prompted by Ted's interest in alpines. The Buchanan Simpsons had acquired their stock from Richard and Susan Stoker, who had cleared land at Cowichan Lake and began a rhododendron collection from seed collected on expeditions. Almost as an afterthought, the Greigs also took the Buchanan Simpsons' species rhododendrons. Mary Greig apparently was unimpressed with them, comparing them to her robust rhododendron hybrids 'Pink Pearl' and 'Britannia'. The Greigs cashed in insurance policies and mortgaged their house to pay for the stock. Moving the plants to Roystan was a task indeed. Ted and

one of the children drove their old car and trailer to Cowichan Lake every weekend for several months. At the end of the road, they shouted across the water to George Buchanan Simpson, who rowed over and picked them up. Thousands of carefully packed three-inch clay pots of alpines were rowed back and stowed away for the 125-mile trip to Royston. Soon, however, the Greigs found that the Royston climate suited the rhododendrons better than the alpines and gradually shifted the focus of their nursery to genus *Rhododendron* and other ericaceous plants. Although the Greigs never visited George Fraser because of the difficult route by car and boat to Ucluelet, they corresponded with him.

The Greigs continued to get seed from the Royal Botanic Garden Edinburgh and subscribed to expeditions of Frank Kingdon-Ward and Joseph Rock. In the 1930s, plants were successfully shipped from Sunningdale Nursery in Surrey, England, via the Panama Canal. After World War II, they were shipped by air with inspection at Montreal where they were often badly repacked with missing labels and no soil. The lack of rhododendron literature created problems in identification of species, and the English rating system proved inapplicable to the British Columbia climate, but the Greigs, like true pioneers, persevered. They even applied for membership in the elite British Rhododendron Society, but J. B. Stevenson wrote back, "We do not accept the trade" (Susan Greig Mouat, personal communication).

The nursery required intense labor on the part of both Ted, who worked full-time as a bookkeeper, and Mary, who was caring for four children at home. Ted built three greenhouses, their heating systems, a propagating house, a mist house, and raised beds. He did all the packing and shipping, installed the irrigation system, dug his own peat, ground the mulch, and sterilized and mixed the potting soil. Mary did the propagating by seed or cutting, kept the records, hand watered the plants, weeded, and wrote the nursery catalog. With the advent of heating cables, rooting hormones, and mist, Mary achieved almost one hundred percent success with her cuttings. Years later she remembered the pleasure of "thrusting one's fingers into the sandy rooting medium and gently lifting out sturdy, well-rooted cuttings" (Susan Mouat, personal communication). Of great interest to her was the variation in species seedlings from wild collected seed; she propagated only from the best forms. She kept meticulous records—perhaps learned during her employment at banks before her marriage—and built an impressive library on rhododendrons. She also learned Latin in middle-age to help with her botanical work. One continuing problem the Greigs faced was separating the true species from the natural hybrids— a challenge that rhododendron collectors continue to face today.

After the formation of the American Rhododendron Society in 1944, of which the Greigs were charter members, they attended its annual conventions, meeting other nurserymen and discussing new growing techniques. They were given the society's Gold Medal Award in 1966, the year that Ted died. One of their greatest pleasures was sharing their knowledge and plants. A donation of a thousand plants formed the basis of the Asian Gardens at the University of British Columbia in Vancouver. Others were donated to Playfair Park in Saanich and the garden at the University of Victoria. By the mid 1960s, with Ted's failing health, the Greigs were ready to sell their nursery. The Vancouver Parks Board agreed to buy the stock and hired Alleyne Cook to manage the collection, which was established in Vancouver's Stanley Park. Among the collection are Mary Greig's *Rhododendron auriculatum* crosses.

The rhododendron hybrids and species selections introduced, registered, grown, or hybridized by Ted and Mary Greig are; 'Buchanan Simpson' (*R. oreodoxa* var. *fargesii* x unknown); 'Butterball' (*R. xanthostephanum* x *R. triflorum*); 'Canada' (*R. campylogynum?* x unknown); *R. pseudochrysanthum* 'Chancellor's Choice'; *R. forrestii* ssp. *forrestii* 'Cyril Berkeley'; 'Edith Berkeley' (*R. sanguineum* ssp. *sanguineum* var. *didymoides* x [*R. auriculatum* x 'Loderi King George']); 'Last Rose' (*R. fortunei* ssp. *discolor* x 'Tally Ho'); 'Mary Greig' (*R. neriiflorum* ssp. *neriiflorum* x *R. souliei*); 'Royal Anne' ('Azor' x unnamed hybrid); 'Royston Festival' (*R. auriculatum* x *R. kyawi*); 'Royston Reverie' (*R. auriculatum* x Fabia Group); 'Royston Rose' ('Last Rose' x *R. auriculatum*); 'Royston Summertime' (*R. auriculatum* x 'Last Rose'); 'Ted Greig' (*R. griersonianum* x unnamed hybrid)?; 'Veronica Milner' (*R. campylocarpum* x 'Little Ben').

Although Fraser and the Greigs worked in virtual isolation from the rest of the rhododendron world, the Layritz Nursery in Victoria was beginning to introduce species and hybrids to the public. Richard Layritz, born in Dresden, Germany, in 1867, and trained in horticulture in Stuttgart, arrived in Victoria in 1889 to start a nursery. When he needed money to expand, he joined the rush to the Klondike and actually returned with gold. Layritz supplied the public with fruit trees for the Okanagan in the province's interior, roses to gardeners, and innumerable trees and shrubs, including some 300 varieties of rhododendrons. He was known as colorful and competent—and unwilling to sell plants to anyone he thought would not take care of them.

The first West Coast rhododendron growers were horticultural pioneers in the truest sense, discovering the adaptability of the genus for a new land and unlocking the mysteries of its propagation with great excitement. Often they were European trained in horticultural skills, bringing with them a long tradition of sound practices and connections with Old World horticulturists. With great hunger, they reached out to their European contemporaries for information on the genus and seed from newly discovered varieties. They were passionate in their quest and dedicated to sharing their good news with the gardening public.

Scattered from British Columbia to southern California, these rhododendron pioneers were largely isolated from each other, depending on their ties to the Old World for information and support. But inevitably they began talking to each other. Through their convergence, a creative West Coast rhododendron milieu was inevitable, the results of which these pioneers could never have dreamed.

Goheen

Queen Elizabeth Park, Vancouver, B.C.

Strybing Arboretum

Golden Gate Park

CHAPTER 3

THE PUBLIC ARBORETA

The West Coast public arboreta brought their professional staffs and hosts of volunteers into the lively pursuit of rhododendrons. With enthusiasm as keen as the commercial nurserymen's, these scientists added botanical, taxonomic, and horticultural expertise to the growing body of knowledge of the genus. Although initially isolated from their West Coast counterparts in the nursery business, the arboretum professionals inevitably began communicating with those who shared a common passion, no matter what level, and plunged into the mainstream.

GOLDEN GATE PARK AND THE STRYBING ARBORETUM

As with other rhododendron aficionados on the West Coast, the arboreta professionals turned first to the British for information on the genus. In the late 1880s, Sir Joseph Hooker visited the newly appointed superintendent of Golden Gate Park in San Francisco, John McLaren, and convinced him the site, located in USDA Zone 10a, was ideal for rhododendrons. Hooker sent McLaren a collection of plants including *Rhododendron maddenii*, *R. falconeri*, and *R. thomsonii* to be added to the small existing species collection of *R. catawbiense*, *R. maximum*, *R. ponticum*, *R. dalhousiae*, and *R. hodgsonii*. By 1893, forty-four species and hybrids grew in the park. Among the hybrids were 'Aurora', 'Countess of Sefton', and 'Duchess of Connaught'.

Strybing Arboretum

John McLaren

In spite of the destruction of park properties by campers made homeless by the Great Fire, in 1910 eighty-six rhododendron hybrids and species still thrived. At about this time the lovely hybrid 'Fragrantissimum' was added and soon after came 'Pink Pearl', *R. griffithianum* and *R. cinnabarinum*.

In 1915, John McLaren landscaped the Panama Pacific Exposition in San Francisco where the Japanese Kurume azaleas so inspired the Domoto family of nurserymen. McLaren was determined to produce the finest show of rhododendrons ever seen in America. Hybrids from Belgium, Holland, and England, included 'Cornubia', 'Loderi', 'Cynthia', and 'Lady

Clementine Mitford'. After the exposition, McLaren dramatically massed the rhododendrons beneath Monterey pine and cypress on the banks of a path leading through a dell in Golden Gate Park.

McLaren felt adamantly that the natural woodland setting of the dell should not be "marred" by monuments. According to park lore, after a life-size monument of McLaren was created he hid it under a mattress in the park stable. No one found it until after his death when it was, ironically, placed in the new Rhododendron Dell.

The climate of San Francisco, with its mild winters and foggy summers, suited the tender Himalayan hybrids better than the English climate, where they were often relegated to the

Brydon

Percy Hadden "Jock" Brydon

greenhouse. The hybrids 'Lady Alice Fitzwilliam', 'Gibsonii', 'Exoniense', 'Countess of Haddington', 'Forestianum', 'Princess Alice', and 'Sesterianum' thrived in the park. Many of the tender species from subsection *Maddenia* were also grown, including *R. burmanicum, R. ciliatum, R. formosum, R. veitchianum, R. maddenii, R. dalhousiae, R. lindleyi, R. nuttallii, R. taggianum*

The construction of the Kezar Stadium in the park forced the moving of McLaren's rhododendron plantings to sites throughout the park, many to the DeLaveagar Dell, where new British hybrids were planted as they arrived but, sadly, were frequently stolen by greedy collectors. After McClaren's death in 1943, an assistant park superintendent, Roy Hudson, supervised the plantings for the John McLaren

Memorial Rhododendron Dell created to honor McLaren who, among the many plants in his care, loved rhododendrons most of all.

Today the Rhododendron Dell collection includes many species, numerous azaleas, and old English hybrids, among them 'Cynthia', 'Pink Pearl', 'Cilpinense', 'Cornubia', 'Mrs. Tom H. Lowinsky', 'Unknown Warrior', 'Mrs. G. W. Leak', 'Loder's White', 'The Honourable Jean Marie de Montague', and the Naomi Group. A substantial number of species rhododendrons from subsection *Maddenia* and their hybrids grace the collection with their voluptuous flowers and fragrance, among them: *Rhododendron veitchianum, R. dalhousiae, R. formosum, R. burmanicum*, 'Forsterianum', 'Lady Alice Fitzwilliam', 'Countess of Haddington', and 'My Lady' and 'Mi Amor' by Maurice Sumner. A

American Rhododendron Society Files

Peter Cox (2nd from left) and Jock Brydon (far right)

number of the subsection *Maddenia* hybrids of Bob Scott also appear. In addition, are hardy West Coast hybrids, among them: 'Taurus' by Frank Mossman and 'Red Walloper' and 'Lem's Cameo' by Halfdan Lem.

In 1961, P. H. Brydon, director of the Strybing Arboretum at Golden Gate Park, introduced vireya rhododendrons to the rhododendron collection. The National Arboretum in Washington, D. C., supplied the first plants, and collections by Dr. Hermann Sleumer supplied the bulk of the species collection. Brydon, who himself explored their natural habitat in the Malay Archipelago, started a program of testing and hybridizing these tender plants in a greenhouse and interested a number of amateur horticulturists in them, most notably Peter Sullivan of San Francisco. During the winter months especially, visitors enjoyed the color and fragrance of the vireya flowers. At the time of their introduction at Strybing the vireyas were considered "one of the most prom-

ising groups of untried plants suitable for growing in Coastal California" (Sullivan 1972). When it was time to plant the collection outside, a protected area provided an ideal spot. Although some of the epiphytic species were difficult, success with various terrestrial species proved promising, among them: *Rhododendron laetum*, *R. phaeopeplum*, *R. leucogigas*, and *R. javanicum*. Unfortunately, subsequent freezes badly damaged the collection. However, Brydon's and his successors' interest in the vireyas, along with Peter Sullivan and other amateurs in California, kindled an enthusiasm for vireyas that would not die.

Bovees Nursery

'Marudu Bay'

Bovees Nursery

'Doris Mossman'

Bovees Nursery

R. laetum

Himalayan Area
University of California
Botanical Gardens, Berkeley

University of California, Berkeley

UNIVERSITY OF CALIFORNIA BOTANICAL GARDENS, BERKELEY

In Strawberry Canyon in the Berkeley hills, facing San Francisco Bay to the west and shaded by a canopy of California live oaks, the University of California Botanical Gardens amassed a rhododendron collection that grew to some 250 species by 1945, including both Asian and North American. In 1930 Joseph Rock visited the garden and was so impressed with the collection, which numbered about 100, that he proposed that the university sponsor a plant hunting expedition to China and Tibet for rhododendron seed. The expedition added greatly to the interest in the garden's Rhododendron Dell. By 1945, Jack Whitehead, manager of the garden, reported that thirty-five of the total forty-four rhododendron series (using the old series classification) were represented.

University of California, Berkeley

U.C. Botanical Gardens, Berkeley

Philp

Mendocino Coast Botanical Gardens

MENDOCINO COAST BOTANICAL GARDENS

When Ernest Shoefer began what is now the Mendocino Coast Botanical Gardens in 1961 near Fort Bragg, he made the rhododendron the signature plant of the gardens, recognizing the climate was ideal for growing a wide range of plants in the genus. Bob Boddy of Descanso Nursery in Fort Bragg gave him many hundreds of rhododendrons, which today are the largest and most stately ones in the gardens. The California Coastal Conservancy purchased the property in 1982.

The site offers a unique refuge for tender rhododendrons that dislike hard freezes but like the moisture-laden air moving in from the ocean and the shade from a high canopy of pine. The region is home to natives *Rhododendron macrophyllum* and *R. occidentale*, but emphasis in the gardens is on tender exotic species and hybrid rhododendrons that are intolerant of colder climates further north. (The gardens lie within USDA Zone 9b with average minimum temperatures from 30°f to 25°F [-1.2°C to -3.8°C].) In the garden canyons, the environment is similar to that found by Frank Kingdon-Ward in Burma, with streams, ferns, and rhododendrons growing on mountainsides beneath a protective canopy.

The Fort Bragg Rhododendron Section of the gardens includes both old named and unnamed hybrids of the region and new named hybrids. Many of the newer hybrids bear the names "Pomo", "Noyo", and "Fort Bragg" in their names (Philp, personal communication).

WASHINGTON PARK ARBORETUM

Further north, in the Puget Sound area of Western Washington (USDA Zone 8b), another large arboretum reached out to the East Coast, Europe and Asia for rhododendrons to add to its collection of woody plants. Soon after its establishment in 1934, the Washington Park Arboretum in Seattle, affiliated with the University of Washington, began collecting rhododendrons. By the end of the 1940s, some fifty species and thirty hybrids had been planted. The species included *Rhododendron augustinii, R. auriculatum, R. brachycarpum, R. calostrotum, R. cinnabarinum, R. canescens, R. dauricum, R. decorum, R. fortunei, R. mucronulatum,* and *R. oreotrephes* among others. 'Azor', 'Bow Bells', 'Britannia', 'Christmas Cheer', Fraseri Group, 'John Wister', 'Loder's White', 'Pink Pearl', and 'Purple Splendour' were among the hybrids.

University of Washington

Washington Park Arboretum

One of the features of the arboretum, designed by Frederick L. Olmsted, was Azalea Way, a wide grassy path adorned on both sides with sumptuous beds of evergreen azaleas.

Joy Spur

Azalea Way, Washington Park Arboretum

In 1946, the newly formed Seattle Rhododendron Society (later to become the Seattle Chapter of the American Rhododendron Society) held the first Annual Rhododendron Show at the arboretum, under the chairmanship of Donald G. Graham. Three thousand people visited the show, held in a tent 70 feet by 25 feet (21 x 7.5 m). Among the judges for the show were West Coast rhododendron experts P. H. Brydon and Theodore Van Veen, Sr. Donald Graham himself won prizes with a bright orange truss of 'Lady Chamberlain' and a pink-orange truss of 'Lady Rosebery', both with *Rhododendron cinnabarinum* in its parentage, and with trusses of the species *R. neriiflorum* and *R. campylocarpum*.

Brian Mulligan

The arboretum staff and members of the Seattle Rhododendron Society joined efforts to provide the public with a dramatic display of the genus that would win the hearts of Washington gardeners for decades to come.

Brian O. Mulligan, appointed director of the Washington Park Arboretum in 1946, greatly increased the rhododendron collection during his tenure. Among the plantings was the collection of the Loderi Group whose site would become the arboretum's Loderi Valley, where the rhododendrons grew to tree size and in bloom scented the protected ravine with sublime fragrance.

Under Mulligan's tenure as director, the American Rhododendron Hybrid Garden was developed under arboretum curator Joseph A. Witt. The garden would feature American rhododendron hybrids by well-known hybridizers of the time: Charles Dexter, Joseph Gable, Guy Nearing, P. J. Mezitt and other East Coast hybridizers and West Coast hybridizers John Bacher, Robert Bovee, Edgar Greer, John and Rudolph Henny, Carl Phetteplace, Theodore Van Veen, Sr., Lester Brandt, James Caperci, Halfdan Lem, William Whitney and others. The site would include dwarf, medium and tall rhododendrons placed aesthetically on a sloping plot under magnolias and other trees. During the 1980s, however, shortage of funds resulted in the garden's decline, and by 1996 only thirty-five rhododendrons remained in a deteriorating jungle of growth. However, in 1990 a memorial planting to honor Dr. Herschel Roman, a plant geneticist at the University of Washington, was developed to show genetics at work. A section of the garden was devoted to showing the parentage of one of the most well known of Puget Sound hybrids, 'Lem's Cameo', a cross by Halfdan Lem. Along with 'Lem's Cameo' were planted its parents, a selection from the Dido Group and 'Anna'. The planting inspired the arboretum to re-think the focus of the garden. In 1996, a new arboretum mission state-

Dunn Estate

Edward B. Dunn

ment included the development of a Puget Sound Rhododendron Hybrid Garden to replace the American Rhododendron Garden and feature the many crosses of a growing number of Puget Sound hybridizers.

Edward Dunn and Brian Mulligan were largely responsible for the Seattle Rhododedron Society acquiring the Meerkerk Rhododendron Gardens on Whidbey Island in 1982. Dunn, president of the University of Washington Arboretum in 1960, presided over the opening of the Japanese Garden there. Active in the early group of rhododendron enthusiasts who eventually formed the Rhododendron Species Foundation, Ed Dunn was very instrumental in the establishment of the Species Foundation garden at Federal Way, Washington.

Dunn's 2½ acre garden was his pride and joy, revealing his enjoyment of hybridizing rhododendrons, collecting and growing woodland wildflowers. He combined these plants with water features and trees to encourage wildlife and delight visitors. His gardening philosophy is preserved in the Edward B. Dunn Historical Garden, established in 1993.

Largely through the efforts of Brian O. Mulligan, the Washington Park Arboretum had joined the rhododendron ground swell.

UNIVERSITY OF BRITISH COLUMBIA BOTANICAL GARDEN

At the University of British Columbia in Vancouver, the collecting of rhododendrons began in the 1930s when approximately a dozen hardy Dutch rhododendron hybrids were planted around one of the old buildings on campus. At that time it was believed that only *Rhododendron ponticum* and its hybrids were hardy enough to thrive in the Vancouver climate (USDA Zone 8b). Time and experience, however, proved that the climate was conducive to growing a wide range of species and hybrids and lead to the creation of a magnificent collection of Asian species.

The impetus to start a rhododendron collection at the university began in 1952 with a donation of species from Ted and Mary Greig of Royston. Within two years the collection reached 1,000 plants, and soon the university was exchanging seeds with other botanical gardens. In the early 1950s, Nick Weesjes, a member of the university's Botanical Garden staff, raised thousands of species seedlings from the Royal Botanic Garden,

Edinburgh, and other gardens, although once the plants matured, the staff realized not all were the species they were supposed to be. This problem undoubtedly influenced the University to join with the fledging Rhododendron Species Foundation in 1964 to raise species from cuttings sent from Britain. Because of government import restrictions, the Rhododendron Species Foundation in Tacoma, Washington, could not import plants from Britain and other European countries. Since the Canadian government had no such restrictions, the cuttings were sent to the University of British Columbia, rooted in Canada, and then sent across the border to the United States. In exchange for raising the cuttings, the University was allowed to keep cuttings of each species for its own collection.

The propagation skills of Nick Weesjes and Evelyn Jack, another University staff member (who would become Evelyn Weesjes after her marriage to Nick), were highly respected. In a letter from Mary Greig to the supervisor of grounds at the University, she said, "If Nick and Evelyn can't get results, no one else is likely to!" (Barrett 1994).

The 17-acre David C. Lam Asian Garden, a part of the older Botanical Garden at the University, with its emphasis on Asian genera *Rhododendron*, *Magnolia*, *Rosa*, *Sorbus*, and *Hamamelis*, opened in 1983. The growing conditions for

Weesjes

Evelyn and Nick Weesjes

rhododendrons were ideal, protected from wind by a 200-foot (60 m) cliff and blessed with a floor of forest debris. By the 1980s, the Asian Garden contained over 440 species, some of them rare in cultivation. Represented are specimens of subsection *Grandia*, and microclimates enable *R. griffithianum* and *R. edgeworthii* to survive—a far cry from the original collection limited to hardy hybrids and *R. ponticum*. A magnificent specimen of *R. argyrophyllum* ssp. *nankingense* 'Chinese Silver', with silver indumentum, dark green rugulose leaves, and clear pink flowers is a sight to behold. Also in the garden are a dark pink form of *R. metternichii*, selected forms of *R. wardii*, a white form of *R. smirnowii*, and a deep blue form of *R. augustinii*. Nearby, the Alpine Garden contains many dwarf rhododendron species.

Besides its connection with the Rhododendron Species Foundation in Washington, the University of British Columbia Botanical Garden staff was in close contact with Washington hybridizers Hjalmar Larson of Tacoma during the 1960s, who gave the staff some fifty of his crosses to grow on. Larson visited once or twice a year to evaluate them. Among the named crosses were 'Buttered Popcorn', 'Hazel Fisher', 'Hjalmar L. Larson', and 'Lemon Marmalade'.

Evelyn Weesjes recalled an incident when Larson and Elmer Fisher came to the University to pick up his selected crosses: "We had about eighty plants ready for loading, and I was dumbfounded when they arrived in Elmer's small panel vehicle, having expected a good sized truck. But I underestimated Elmer's ingenuity, and all the plants were shoe-horned into that small panel and off they went" (Weesjes, personal communication).

By the 1960s, the University of British Columbia horticultural staff had strong and fruitful relationships with rhododendron enthusiasts south of the border.

In the 1970s, John Bond, Keeper of the Garden at Windsor Great Park in England, visited the Pacific Northwest and was so impressed with new North American hybrids that Lillian Hodgson of Vancouver arranged to have cuttings from her own collection and from the University of British Columbia Botanical Garden collection sent to him. Hodgson recalled: "I shipped gladly at my own expense over 3,000 scions for it was a joy to return a favour to a country that had so generously shared their plants in the past. Two world wars had prevented any serious hybridizing and this presented an opportunity to introduce new blood. It was not without some bureaucratic interference in which the large boxes, though air freighted, were held unnecessarily, until I placed a few radiation stickers on them and future shipments arrived in record time" (Hodgson, personal communication). The generosity in the world of rhododendrons was thus practiced on both sides of the Atlantic.

Alleyne Cook of North Vancouver, British Columbia, helped develop several rhododendron heritage gardens, including the Greig Rhododendron Garden in Vancouver's Stanley Park. For his contributions, the American Rhododendron Society awarded him the Gold Medal in 1999.

RHODODENDRON SPECIES FOUNDATION

In Oregon, frustration gave birth to the Rhododendron Species Foundation, which would in time establish a world-class collection of species rhododendrons. In spite of overwhelming obstacles, the foundation eventually developed a rhododendron species botanical garden in Federal Way, Washington, as an invaluable public arboretum for the display, preservation, and distribution of species.

It all began as the West Coast interest in species rhododendrons grew and the difficulty in finding true species became apparent. All too often, open-pollinated seed from both Britain and the United States produced plants that were either hybrids or inferior forms of the species. Increasing the confusion was the often-conflicting literature describing the species. The situation was particularly frustrating for hybridizers who wanted good forms of true species for their crosses.

In 1961, an Oregon physician, Dr. Milton Walker, led a search, under the auspices of the Species Project of the American Rhododendron Society and its president, Dr. J. Harold Clarke,

Rhododendron Species Foundation

Milton V. Walker, M.D.
1903-1986

to find the best forms of true species in the Pacific Northwest. Walker had recently retired from his medical practice and the operation of his clinic and become absorbed in the genus *Rhododendron* at his home in Pleasant Hill, near Eugene, Oregon. The first step was to locate where species were grown and by whom. The ten species selected for the project were: *Rhododendron souliei, R. wardii, R. calophytum, R. oreodoxa* ssp. *fargesii* (at the time known as *R. fargesii*), *R. haematodes, R. sanguineum* ssp. *didymum* (at the time known as *R. didymum*), *R. barbatum, R. strigillosum, R. augustinii,* and *R. hippophaeoides.* Sent out like detectives to inspect gardens in all kinds of weather was a committee composed of Arthur Childers of Eugene, Merle Cisney of Portland, Ben Nelson of Seattle, Charles Edmund of Tacoma, and others. Once the species were located, however, puzzles arose. For instance, the authoritative book at the time, *The Species of Rhododendrons* by J. B. Stevenson of Tower Court, England, described *R. haematodes* with an obovate or oblong shape. Yet the so-called Exbury form of the species found in West Coast gardens had an elliptic shape. Was the Exbury form a hybrid or a form of the species? Mind-boggling questions arose.

In his report of the work of the Species Project, Walker wrote: "Even the recognition of plants truly representative of their species is not always a simple matter. It may be that there are certain variations from the described characteristics of a species that we will have to recognize by describing different forms of the typical species. But just how much variation from the published botanical description will be permissible? These and other questions that have arisen are making the species study stimulating and exciting" (Walker 1962).

These enthusiastic rhododendron sleuths, searching for the telling characteristics of the true species, faced puzzles that rhododendron taxonomists would spend a lifetime of scientific study

unraveling. Although they failed to describe the typical true species, they did manage to identify many fine forms, such as a *R. calophytum* grown by James Barto, a *R. thomsonii* grown by Ralph C. Jacobson, and a *R. metternichii* grown by Hjalmar Larson. Because of the difficulty in identifying true species, Walker and his sleuths changed their objective to finding superior forms of the species.

The frustration in identifying the characteristics of a true rhododendron species on the basis of plants in West Coast Gardens prompted Walker to visit English rhododendron collections in 1964 to see which species forms the British had selected as "best" and, if possible, produce cuttings. Walker must have been busy indeed on that trip, for his list of best species included plants from many gardens. He also became acquainted with numerous British collectors and staff members of botanic gardens. At the same time he conceived of the idea of a species rhododendron garden of the best forms, both from Britain and North America.

Walker's fellow species enthusiast, Wales Wood of St. Helens, Oregon, writes that the idea for the foundation began one day in Towercourt: "During the spring of 1960, Mrs. Wood and I had the opportunity of spending considerable time in the rhododendron gardens of Scotland and England and with the great people associated with these gardens. We were impressed with the quality of the rhododendron species in these gardens and we thought it was so unfortunate that so many rather ordinary hybrids had been imported into the USA and so few of the fine species. It was on this same visit to England in the garden at Towercourt and in our presence that Mrs. Stevenson made the comment about growing species from seed to Dr. Carl Phetteplace, which observation Dr. Milton Walker gives credit for the formation of the Rhododendron Species Foundation. Really, I have always felt that the purchase of a very inferior plant of *R. strigillosum* at a rather large price had as much to do with the formation of the Foundation. The plant was a very bad form both in foliage and color of bloom, bereft of bristles and a dirty pink in color of bloom. Dr. Walker is a person who likes to get value received for his money" (Barrett 1994).

If Walker's dream was to come true, the cuttings of the "best forms" could not be sent directly to the United States because law required fumigation of plant material. Since Canada did not require fumigation, Walker began communication with Herman Vaartnou, supervisor of grounds at the University of British Columbia. Arrangements were made to have the cuttings sent to the University where staff member Evelyn Jack would propagate and care for them for two years. They were to be sent on Mondays to arrive before the weekend. Although they sometimes arrived wilted, they were capable of being revived for propagation under Evelyn Jack's skillful hand. In return for the work, the University would keep a selection of all the species propagated.

In 1965, Dr. J. Harold Clarke laid out the situation to members of the American Rhododendron Society in an article in the society's *Quarterly Bulletin*. He emphasized the importance of finding superior species forms and the establishment of a garden where they could be grown, seen, and purchased by the public. He also made it clear that the American Rhododendron Society was not financially able to support such a project. He announced that a non-profit Rhododendron Species Foundation had been incorporated in the state of Oregon and that $1 million would be needed to support the project, to be raised through donations. The Species Project was now on its own, under Walker's presidency. Other founding members of the foundation were: Wales Wood,

vice president; Fred M. Robbins, secretary; Dr. J. Harold Clarke, director; Edward B. Dunn, director; and Cecil Smith, director.

Although the rhododendron cuttings were already growing at the University of British Columbia, the newly formed foundation had virtually no money to support them and no garden in which to grow them. The challenges were great, indeed, for the fledgling foundation, but a core group of people refused to let go of the dream. Ruth M. Woods describes their early meetings: "Meetings were always very informal—sort of a family affair. In most instances both husband and wife were so active that no one paid any attention to which one was listed as director. You could discuss RSF business with Helen or Milton, Molly or Cecil, Fred or Dorothy, Jock or Edith" (Barrett 1994).

Large scale fund raising for the project ran amok when potential large benefactors insisted on assurance that the garden would be permanent with enough funds for its maintenance. However, with an empty treasury, the foundation was barely able to pay its modest administrative bills. Walker had become so discouraged that he wrote Evelyn Jack that instead of a garden for the plants she had propagated, they would be transported to the United States and dispersed to the public through a wholesale nursery.

Then, in 1968, Walker and his wife, Helen, made a generous offer to sell their property in Pleasant Hill to the foundation, and the foundation board agreed to buy it. The bulk of the financing was carried by foundation board members and others closely related to the project. (An estimated $18,000 a year was needed to retire the indebtedness of the property and maintain the garden.) In the fall of that year, some 800 plants were moved from Vancouver to Pleasant Hill in an 18-foot van. Despite a broken water pump on the van and delays at U.S. Customs, the little plants survived the second big journey of their lives. Although a major hurdle had been overcome, the foundation's lack of finances made it increasingly difficult to fulfill its financial obligations to the Walkers.

The failure of the foundation to raise enough money to buy the property and maintain the garden greatly disillusioned Walker after the immense effort and money he had invested to collect the species and maintain them on his own property. Through action by the foundation directors, the garden property was returned to the Walkers and a new site was found in Salem. At this point in the rocky history of the foundation, a man appears with strong ties to the Strybing Arboretum in San Francisco: P. H. "Jock" Brydon.

Brydon was born in Scotland in 1906 and studied horticulture and botany at the East of Scotland College of Agriculture. In 1927 he moved to the United States and worked first for a New York seed company and later for seed and wholesale florist companies in California. In 1932 he was hired by the University of California Botanical Gardens in Berkeley where he propagated seed from Joseph Rock's expeditions to China. During his ten-year tenure he developed the Strawberry Canyon Rhododendron Dell at the gardens. At the same time he was active in the founding of the California Horticultural Society in San Francisco and edited the *California Horticultural Quarterly*. Because his training had not prepared him to advance to the directorship of

Adams

Rhododendron Species Foundation Gazebo in winter

the University of California Botanical Gardens, Brydon and his wife, Edith, moved first to Lompoc, California, where he again worked for a seed company and then to Granger, Washington, where they grew cherries, apricots, and peaches. In 1946, the Brydons moved to Salem, Oregon, where he joined in partnership with John Henny in growing rhododendrons. He later started his own nursery, Brydon's Nursery and Seed Store, in Salem, which had exclusive rights to plants from the Rothschild's Exbury Estate. During these years he often lectured, displaying a beguiling sense of humor, and wrote numerous articles. Then, in 1960, he returned to California as director of the Strybing Arboretum for ten years. In 1970 the Brydons returned to Salem

where they bought a 20-acre cherry orchard—the orchard that was to become the new home for the foundation's rhododendrons.

During a rainy, cold April in 1970, Jock Brydon and others began hauling plants from the Walkers' lath house to the Brydon home near Salem. Some 2,000 plants were dug and lined out temporarily in nursery beds. At this point the collection included 515 accessions, with a total of 384 species, subspecies, and selected clones. The collection was eventually to be planted under a canopy of garry oak, madrone, and Douglas fir. As propagation facilities were expanded, Brydon increased the numbers of cuttings for distribution. The Brydons devoted themselves full-time to the collection, hiring workers to care

Adams

Rhododendron Species Foundation Rock Garden

for their cherry orchard! In spite of a killing freeze in December 1971, Brydon and his wife, Edith, dramatically increased the number of propagated species, and these, along with increased accessions, forced the foundation again to look for a larger site for the collection.

In 1973, Brydon and two other foundation members, Treasurer Corydon Wagner and President Fred Robbins, met for the first time with George Weyerhaeuser of the Weyerhaeuser Corporation. They requested that the corporation provide a site for the collection at its headquarters in Federal Way. The Weyerhaeuser Corporation embraced the idea and gave the foundation use of twenty-four acres of native woodland. Brydon and his Salem volunteers dug, balled, and burlapped some 2,000 plants for the move. At Brydon's recommendation, a garden manager was hired—29-year-old Kendall Gambrill. At the same time, donations increased, an endowment fund was established, the directors changed the bylaws to include a general membership as opposed to an exclusive membership of contributors of large sums, and the number of garden volunteers increased. The Rhododendron Species Foundation had survived, along with a very well-traveled collection of rhododendrons.

After the move to Federal Way, Jock Brydon continued his involvement with the foundation and suggested various options for organizing the rhododendrons in the garden: taxonomically, geographically by region of origin, or culturally. When the foundation drew up its first master plan in 1977, Brydon urged it to employ a garden director who, among his or her many duties, would authenticate species.

In an article in the *Washington Park Arboretum Bulletin* in 1976, author Doris Butler wrote glowingly about the garden: "What is important about the garden is that here will be room for only the top forms. Every form planted will be an A.M. (Award of Merit) form earned against competition, or a top form from private and public gardens of the British Isles, Japan, American or elsewhere, or that obtained from today's plant hunters, for some feel that many species remain to be discovered. Each plant will typify the finest form available. All will be forms recognized as authentic species; all will have been keyed or identified by authorities. . . . Nothing like it exists anywhere in the world" (Barrett 1994).

The continuing concern among foundation members, especially Walker, was the question of authentic species. Experts from around the world had visited the garden to confirm the species: H. H. Davidian, Peter Cox, Koichiro Wada, M. N. and W. R. Philipson, Brian O. Mulligan, and Brydon himself. Protecting the authenticity of collection and, hence, the integrity of the foundation was top priority. Walker was adamant about not repeating the mistakes of the British seed exchanges that distributed seed of unauthenticated species worldwide. He also testily accused the American Rhododendron Society seed exchange of doing the same thing. Even plants from the gardens of foundation members were suspect and would be placed in a special section called the "Founders Garden," separate and apart from the original collection.

So careful was the foundation in protecting its integrity regarding the distribution of good forms of true species that it turned down a proposal by garden manager Ken Gambrill to start a seed exchange. However, seed collected in the wild was grown on at the garden and seed and seedlings disbursed to other botanical gardens.

Although the foundation was adding the accouterments of a public arboretum, such as a library and educational programs, the foundation's internal structure of president, executive committee, board of directors and staff, and the line of command were unclear. As a result, personal conflicts arose. For instance, a bitter dispute arose over who should decide how much nitrogen to use to break down the sawdust that had been spread over the site as a growing medium.

In spite of the growth in membership, increased endowment fund donations, and development of the garden, financial crises continued to plague the foundation. But in 1980 the first executive director, Richard Piacentini, announced that the foundation was in the best financial position ever, with operating income exceeding expenses, the award of grants, and a healthy endowment fund.

Under the leadership of its presidents—Milton Walker, Wales Wood, Edward Dunn, Fred Robbins, Lawrence Pierce, William Hatheway, Jane Rogers, David Goheen, Esther Berry, Herbert Spady, David Jewell, Burt Mendlin, Don King, Fred Whitney, and Honoré

Hacanson—the foundation has gained stability and a worldwide reputation for the collection, display, and distribution of good forms of true rhododendron species.

The Rhododendron Species Foundation, along with the other West Coast public arboreta, added a substantial layer of professional staffs and vigorous volunteers to the momentum of interest in the genus *Rhododendron*. By the mid 1940s, from California to British Columbia, islands of rhododendron enthusiasts on all levels—hobbyist, commercial, and professional—burned with the desire to learn more about the genus, collect its best specimens, and spread the word to the public. The next step inevitably was the formation of an organization to better achieve their goals.

CHAPTER 4

THE AMERICAN RHODODENDRON SOCIETY

By the 1940s, the intense interest in the genus *Rhododendron* among the various groups of the West Coast horticultural community–nurserymen, amateur hybridizers, arboretum professionals, and the public–demanded a channel for its expression. From the start, these rhododendron zealots reached out to others on the West Coast, East Coast, Europe, and even Asia for information and kindred spirits. The Rhododendron Association in Britain had functioned as such a channel, but its distance from the West Coast and its hiatus during World War II called for an organization more responsive to North American and, specifically, West Coast needs. On the East Coast as early as 1931, Guy Nearing wrote to Joseph Gable that an American rhododendron association was needed because of the British preoccupation with war. By 1942, rumblings began on

the West Coast to form an association. Then, in 1944, at the epicenter of rhododendron activity–Portland–a group of people emerged who would take on the task.

THE FOUNDERS

The man the group chose as its leader personified, in many ways, the new organization: John Henny of Brooks, Oregon. Sold on the genus, dedicated to his mission, and affable in demeanor, Henny skillfully rounded up the people who would form the core of a brand new American rhododendron organization.

Van Veen

John Henny

John Henny first encountered rhododendrons in the 1930s, when he and his brother Rudolph and their wives traveled the West Coast during bloom season. They bought ten plants and were hooked for life. They went on to visit nurseries that grew named hybrids, including the Van Veen Nursery and Bernard Esch Nursery in Portland, Endre Ostbo's nursery near Seattle, and the Layritz Nursery in Victoria, British Columbia, through which they also ordered hybrids from British nurseries.

Reaching further afield, John Henny wrote letters to Lionel de Rothschild and Lord Aberconway in Britain for plants, although fumigation with methyl bromide by government officials nearly killed them. He would later meet Edmund de Rothschild in San Francisco and

drive with him to Oregon. Henny recalled the event: "He wanted to see the redwood trees. We spent a night in Medford and the next day fishing the Rogue River. Eddie bet me a silver dollar that he could catch the first fish. I still have the dollar" (Henny 1995). Through his West Coast sojourns and visits to Britain he began to build an interest in forming a new rhododendron association.

Along with John Henny, George D. Grace of Portland helped lay the groundwork for the new organization, traveling with Henny on weekends from Eugene to Seattle in 1942 and 1943. Grace was a Portland homebuilder with a business sense that would prove invaluable in the new organization. Later Grace would help sponsor plant expeditions by Frank Kingdon-Ward and Joseph Rock in Asia. The Grace residence was known for its fine rhododendron plantings, including tree-size Loderi Group specimens, and trusses from his plants often took first prize in shows.

Robinson

George Grace and Joe Gable

On May 29, 1944, a small group of rhododendron growers and collectors met at the home of E. R. Peterson in the West Slope area of Portland to begin to form the organization which had been so much on their minds. They named it the "American Rhododendron Society" and elected John Henny, president; H. G. Ihrig of Seattle, vice president; E. R. Peterson, treasurer; and George D. Grace, secretary. The group held another preliminary meeting on June 20, 1944, and set annual dues at five dollars. They agreed to send letters to interested people to come to the first meeting, pay their five-dollar dues, and become charter members. A total of 160 people joined as charter members, ninety-six from Oregon, forty-four from Washington, three from California, two from British Columbia, and the remaining fifteen from the East Coast and Midwest (see Appendix I).

THE FIRST MEETING

On July 7, 1944, the first meeting of the American Rhododendron Society drew rhododendron enthusiasts from Oregon to Washington to hear the officers speak on the progress of the group. John Henny undoubtedly began the meeting with a joke, a tradition he continued throughout his long involvement with the society. Others who spoke at the first meeting were W. G. Tucker, H. H. Harms, Joe Johnson, and Nick Radovich, all of Portland, and Endre Ostbo of Seattle. John Bacher, however, starred in this first meeting with his color slides. Ruth Hansen of Portland remembers the thrill she felt at seeing the photographs: "As a member of that audience I sat entranced, for it was the

first time I had ever seen pictures of any of the dwarf Lapponicums and these impressed me far more than the large flowered hybrids" (Hansen 1974). Bacher also captivated the audience with the first West Coast showing of a specimen of *Rhododendron bureavii*, which he had grown from seed collected in Asia in 1932. The plant was auctioned off—the first of many hundreds of plants to be auctioned in meetings of the society. The first meeting of the American Rhododendron Society had set the tone for the many meetings to come—fellowship, information, and drama.

ARTICLES OF INCORPORATION

On Jan. 9, 1945, the officers, with P. H. Brydon taking the place of H. G. Ihrig as vice president, signed the society's Articles of Incorporation, which set forth the purposes of the new society, namely:

"To promote and develop the growing of rhododendrons throughout the United States and to associate together in membership persons interested in promoting and developing the growing of rhododendrons.

"To disseminate information relative to the development and culture of rhododendrons; to operate test gardens and exhibition gardens; to catalog named varieties of rhododendrons; to register names of new rhododendron hybrids and in general to do any and all acts or things necessary, convenient or desirable in the promotion and development of the growing and culture of rhododendrons" (American Rhododendron Society 1945).

In the Articles of Incorporation, the new society took its first steps by establishing goals appropriate for a serious horticultural organization.

With great foresight, the founding members first addressed the concept of membership. Democratic from the start, the society was intended to be an association open to anyone interested in rhododendrons. The West Coast rhododendron growers and collectors had already built a loose fellowship among themselves, and now they invited the public to join them in their joyous pursuit. Although the Articles of Incorporation made no mention of chapters, soon members living too far from Portland to attend meetings wanted their own meetings. In 1949, East Coast members held their first meeting in New York City, and members in Seattle and Tacoma began to hold their own meetings. In 1951, the by-laws were revised to include local chapters. The next year the society approved affiliation of the Eugene, Seattle, Tacoma, and California chapters. Portland also organized itself as a chapter. In 1955, the first Canadian chapter, the Vancouver Chapter, was approved. Among its founding members were Lilian Hodgson, David Freeman, Alleyne Cook, and Clive Justice, and later Harold Johnson was influential in starting more British Columbia chapters. One by one, chapters of the American Rhododendron Society formed on the West Coast: in the 1950s, Grays Harbor and Olympic Peninsula chapters; and in the 1960s, Shelton, Olympia, Tualatin, North Kitsap, and Southwestern Oregon chapters. Following these early chapters in Oregon were: Willamette, Siuslaw, and Corvallis chapters; in Washington were: Komo Kulshan, Juan de Fuca, Lewis County, Whidbey Island, Cascade, Pilchuck, and Peninsula chapters; in California were: Southern California, Monterey Bay, DeAnza, Eureka, and Noyo chapters; and in British Columbia were: Victoria,

Fraser Valley, Cowichan Valley, Fraser South, Mt. Arrowsmith, Nanimo, Peace Arch, North Island chapters.

By 2000, West Coast membership in the American Rhododendron Society totaled 2,344, out of a total of 5,766 for the entire society.

PUBLICATIONS

To "disseminate information," the society immediately began spreading the word about rhododendrons through the printed word embellished with photographs. Dean Collins, a charter member and the garden editor of the *Oregon Journal*, served as editor of the first yearbook. The firm Binford & Mort printed all the yearbooks. The year of its incorporation, the society published *The Rhododendron Yearbook for 1945*, the first of five yearbooks printed in the first five years. Inside the front cover of the first yearbook is a color photo of the hybrid 'Mrs. Donald G. Graham' raised by Endre Ostbo, who probably received the seed from England. The real Mrs. Donald G. Graham was, of course, a charter member along with her husband, who chaired the first Seattle rhododendron show to which 3,000 people came. Endre Ostbo, also a charter member, was an avid hybridizer (see Chapter 5). West Coast contributors to the 1945 yearbook include two men who played major roles in creating interest in rhododendrons from the beginning—P. H. Brydon and John Bacher. Brydon wrote the first article in this first ARS publication on rhododendron culture in Great Britain. The article was based on a lecture he gave in 1944 to the society. While the focus of the article is rhododendron culture, Brydon also mentions another topic on his mind: the society's task of organizing a breeding program "to produce better and more colorful hybrids which will be bred to suit our needs on the Pacific Coast" (Brydon 1945). Brydon also contributed two other articles to the first yearbook, one on growing rhododendrons from seed and one on the black vine weevil. John Bacher contributed articles on rhododendrons for the rock garden and the planting of rhododendrons. Endre Ostbo contributed an article on rhododendrons in the woodland, and Rudolph Henny wrote on *Rhododendron auriculatum*. The 1945 yearbook also included a list of hybrid rhododendrons, with ratings, borrowed from the yearbook of the Rhododendron Association of England and a list of rhododendrons that had flowered in the Northwest, borrowed from the bulletin of the University of Washington Arboretum. With the publication of the first yearbook, the new society proved it could draw from a pool of highly literate members to inform—and entertain—its membership.

In *The Rhododendron Yearbook for 1946*, John Bacher reported on the society's first rhododendron show in Portland, Endre Ostbo on rhododendron hybrids, O. E. Holmdahl of Seattle on rhododendrons in the landscape design, W. L. Crissey of Brookings, Oregon, on *Rhododendron occidentale*, and Halfdan Lem of Seattle on grafting rhododendrons. In this yearbook, a list of species from the yearbook of the Rhododendron Association of England was printed.

In *The Rhododendron Yearbook for 1947*, West Coast members continued their contributions: John Henny on English gardens and the society's first show, Dr. Robert Gatke of Salem, Oregon, on a Kingdon-Ward expedition, Howard Slonecker of Oak Grove, Oregon, on the society's new test garden in Portland, P. H. Brydon on species, Rudolph Henny on *Rhododendron falconeri*, Carl S. English, Jr., of Seattle

on classification, and Donald Graham on Seattle's first show. A "stud book" list of hybrids and their parentage was printed from the 1939 yearbook of the Rhododendron Association of England.

The Rhododendron Yearbook for 1948 continued to express the enthusiasm for all aspects of the genus. In *The Rhododendron Yearbook for 1949*, the last to be published, John Bacher reported with flair on the use of dynamite in rhododendron planting, Roy Hudson on rhododendrons in Golden Gate Park, and P. H. Brydon on foundation planting.

In 1947, along with the publishing of the yearbook, the society published the first edition of the *Quarterly Bulletin of the American Rhododendron Society* with Rudolph Henny as editor. Beginning as a single printed page folded in the middle in the style of today's chapter newsletters, the bulletin by 1948 took on the look and substance of a horticultural journal but continued to print news of the society. Because of the cost of printing, the membership was asked to choose between a bulletin and a yearbook. It chose the bulletin, and under the skillful hand of

Robinson

Rudolph Henny

Rudolph Henny, editor until his death in 1963, the bulletin evolved into a first-rate horticultural journal.

Ruth Hansen, secretary-treasurer at the time of his death, recalls Henny's devotion to the bulletin:

"Perhaps his one obsession was to keep the bulletin free from becoming a 'society' magazine as so many other garden publications had become; he therefore steered away from using pictures of individuals as much as possible. He strongly felt that our bulletin should be strictly a publication on rhododendrons, not people, unless they had actually contributed something of importance to the society. . . Mr. Henny's whole life was centered around the ARS and the quarterly bulletin . . . His influence upon the society helped to form its aims, concepts and policies; yet at no time was he ever outspoken, demanding or verbose. It was his nature to sit quietly at all meetings, hearing all sides of an argument; then, in his quiet manner calmly give his opinion" (Hansen 1963).

Upon Rudolph Henny's death, West Coast members continued to edit the *Quarterly Bulletin*, as it was called by then, and the succeeding *Journal American Rhododendron Society*. Dr. J. Harold Clarke of Long Beach, Washington, took over in 1963; P. H. Brydon in 1969; Reuben A. Hatch of Vancouver,

Washington, in 1972; Molly Grothaus of Lake Oswego, Oregon, in 1973; Ed Egan of Tigard, Oregon, in 1978. Then in 1982 Egan developed the format of the new American Rhododendron Society journal with sixty-four pages and greatly expanded use of color pages. In 1985, Adele Jones of Lake Oswego, Oregon, continued the editing of the journal, followed in 1991 by Sonja Nelson of Mount Vernon, Washington. Nelson wrote the text of this book and is author of *Rhododendrons in the Landscape* published in 2000. Most contributors to the publication continued to be members of society, sharing their own techniques on the practical matters of growing rhododendrons, their gardens, their hybridizing efforts, or their knowledge of a species or hybrid. Contributors, in fact, represent the same diversification as the membership—nurserymen, amateurs, and professional horticulturists.

Spady

Herb and Betty Spady

Egan

Fran and Ed Egan

As president of the society from 1995 to 1997, Dr. Herb Spady sensed the importance of the electronic media and its potential for communication among rhododendron aficionados and established the new Electronics Media Committee. The step led to the establishment of the society's homepage (http://www.rhododendron.org) and the *Rhododendron & Azalea Newsletter* (http://members.aol.com/RandANews/news.html) on the Internet. After his term as president, Spady became publisher of the "R&A News" and his wife, Betty, became editor. The contributions of the Spadys to the world of rhododendrons have ranged from active involvement in the Rhododendron Species Foundation to Herb Spady's re-definition of rhododendron hardiness and his own hybridizing. Betty Spady maintained the society's Speakers' Bureau for several years.

RHODODENDRON SHOWS

From the start, spring shows highlighted the rhododendron bloom season and offered members a chance to show the public what a prize the rhododendron was. Before chapters had been established, the society held the first show in Portland in the spring of 1945, which John Bacher reported in the 1946 yearbook. He wrote: "With the nation at war and all manpower in war industries or the armed services and gasoline and travel restrictions in force, the outlook for a successful show was far from promising. The show committee was sold, however, heart and soul and on the desirability of showing the beauty of rhododendrons to the public. With many new introductions from England to be shown for the first time it was felt certain that

ARS Journal Photo

John Henny, Ted Hansen, Howard Slonecker, Cecil Smith, Rudolph Henny and Bob Bovee at an early rhododendron show.

J. G. Bacher

Rhododendron Show—Portland 1948

the extra effort would be worth while" (Bacher 1946). Members brought the plants, fully balled in burlap, to a park on Park Avenue in Portland and, once in place, placed conifer boughs over the burlapped balls. Periodic showers accompanied this elaborate set-up and continued into the next day. On Sunday, May 13, Mother's Day, the sun shone and people filled the park to look at rhododendrons. Over the two-day show, approximately 25,000 people visited the show. "Never had the public seen such an array or rhododendrons in flower and in such a large assortment of hybrids," Bacher wrote (Bacher 1946).

Bacher notes that among the hybrid rhododendrons that particularly impressed the public were: 'Mrs. C. B. van Nes', 'Loderi', 'Beauty of Littleworth', 'Mrs. G. W. Leak', 'Blue Peter', 'Sappho', 'Bow Bells', 'Day Dream', 'Venator', 'Pink Pearl', 'Alice', 'Eureka Maid', 'Unknown Warrior', 'Earl of Athlone', 'Rosamund Millais', 'Mrs. E. C. Stirling', 'Mars', 'Lady Primrose', 'Butterfly', 'Canary', 'Unique', 'Elspeth', and 'Lady Stuart of Wortley'—not an American hybrid among them!

The next year, the newly formed Seattle Rhododendron Society, which would become the Seattle Chapter of the American Rhododendron Society, held its first show, a judged truss show, in a tent at the Washington Park Arboretum, which 3,000 people attended (see Chapter 3).

So encouraged by the positive response by the public to rhododendron shows, in 1948 the society planned an extravaganza of a show. At the Portland Armory, in addition to a judged truss show, flowering rhododendrons were staged along a waterfall that cascaded from the balcony to the lower floor and meandered stream-like until it was pumped back up to the balcony—dramatic, to be sure, but costly too. The show was a financial failure that threw the society into debt. However, in 1949 the society elected an astute businessman, C. I. Sersanous of Portland, for its president. He skillfully guided the society back to financial stability. The annual show, in spite of the overly enthusiastic Portland venture, became a tradition for most chapters.

TEST AND DISPLAY GARDENS

In keeping with its purpose "to operate test gardens and exhibition gardens," the American Rhododendron Society in 1950 began a plan for developing a test garden on city property at Crystal Springs Lake Island in Portland. President

Robinson

Crystal Springs Rhododendron Garden

Bacher

Moving the large forty year old *R.* Cynthia, a gift from Mr. Keyser to the American Rhododendron Society
Test Garden. President C. I. Sersanous and Mr. Keyser in the foreground.

Sersanous, Ted and Ruth Hansen, and John Bacher made the first reconnaissance of the property, a level 4-acre site with rich, loamy soil and a canopy of tall Douglas fir, and Western red cedar and decided it was appropriate for a test garden.

In a talk by John Bacher, chairman of the project, to the society, he said, "Now it is the task of our membership to render assistance so that the project of a true rhododendron garden can be materialized. In this project it is our desire to create a most unique garden devoted to rhododendrons, and also to use a limited amount of companionate plantings to bring out the fullest measure of beauty of the garden" (Bacher 1951). Howard Slonecker's drawings and survey of the site provided a basis for Secretary Ruth Hansen to devise a garden plan.

With the cooperation of the Portland Park Board, which provided a fence around the site, in October of 1951 members began the removal of unwanted trees by chain saw—to the alarm of neighbors who eventually chipped in to help with the clearing when they heard a rhododendron garden was to be built. A past superintendent of the park contributed a 40-foot (12m) specimen of *Rhododendron* 'Cynthia'. In the January 1951 *Quarterly Bulletin*, a photograph captures the planting of this rhododendron behemoth, root ball and all suspended above the truck that brought it to its new home. Both species and hybrids were to be planted, but in Bacher's opinion "the hybrid rhododendrons will above all capture the public's favor with their greater color range and especially by their prevalence in nursery markets" (Bacher 1951).

Van Veen

**Alfred Martin presents Gold Medal Award to
Ruth Hansen.**

Nurseries and members donated many large specimens, and the University of Washington Arboretum under its curator Brian Mulligan donated numerous species grown from seed.

In 1952, members decided to build a rock garden on a steep slope at the north end of the island for dwarf alpine rhododendrons. John Bacher took charge of the project, making clear that he wanted a first-class rockery with "the best rocks obtainable in the region regardless of the distance one must go for them" (Bacher 1953). Bacher, Cecil Smith, and William Murphy trucked seven tons of lava rock from Santiam Pass. To add to these were two loads of 400-pound Oregon City-type rocks and rocks from Green Mountain, Washington. Other members, including Guy Johnson, C. T. Hansen, William

ARS Journal Photo

**J. Harold Clarke, Alfred Martin and Ted Hansen
at the dedication of Jane R. Martin Entrance Garden in 1961.**

Beginning the work at Crystal Springs Rhododendron Garden, from left to right,
Oscar R. Neet, Ruth Hansen, Ted Hansen and Howard Slonecker.

Whitney, Robert Bovee, Howard Slonecker, M. Reddaway, C. I. Sersanous, and Ben Lancaster, helped with this laborious work.

In the next fifty years, the test garden evolved into a first-rate display garden and its name officially changed to the Crystal Springs Rhododendron Garden. Once again, the many levels of the rhododendron community—commercial, professional, and amateur—converged to make the project a success. Alfred Martin helped fund and develop the Jane Martin En-

trance Garden, highlighted by a waterfall with an arching wooden bridge across the gorge leading to it. The Overlook Garden above the lake featured rhododendrons and companions. In Crystal Springs Lake, the Fred Paddison memorial fountain was added. In the original garden on the island, small trees, such as flowering crabapple and flowering cherry, created a sublayer beneath the tall canopy and companions to the many rhododendrons. The original cool house, a Quonset hut, was converted into an exhibit hall for the Portland Chapter's annual shows. Surrounding the exhibit hall are many of the old plantings—'Loderi Venus', 'Loderi King George', 'Beauty of Littleworth', and more. The Peninsula Garden also featured many old plantings, one of which, 'Antoon van Welie', donated by the Van Veen Nursery, was slid down a hill, rafted across the water, and dragged into place (Jones 1992).

The current chairman of the Crystal Springs Rhododendron Garden, Ted Van Veen, has instigated more improvements—an entrance gateway and a path to the High Bridge.

Other chapters besides the Portland Chapter developed display and test gardens for their beloved rhododendrons, always with an eye for drawing the public in to experience the charm and beauty of the plants.

In 1945 in Eugene, Oregon, Del James' garden was overflowing its borders. He asked the city if he might plant some rhododendrons at the edge of Hendricks Park, which bordered his property, and the city agreed. Then, in 1950, the project expanded when Marshall Lyons and Dr. Royal Gick of Eugene requested of the city that a portion of Hendricks Park be developed to display rhododendrons that modern home sites could not accommodate. Rhododendrons were planted under a canopy of Douglas fir and oak. One feature was the Barto Walk planted with Barto rhododendrons. By 1951, the Eugene Chapter of the American Rhododendron Society formed out of the informally organized Men's Camellia & Rhododendron Society in Eugene, with a display garden already in progress.

Robert

Hendricks Park, Eugene, Oregon

Chapter display and test gardens often evolve from private rhododendron collections. Such was the case with the Seattle Chapter's Meerkerk Rhododendron Gardens, located on Whidbey Island, Washington. Max and Ann Meerkerk moved to Whidbey Island in 1963 and became so enamored of the wild *Rhododendron macrophyllum* growing in profusion on the island that they began planting rhododendrons on their property. Their search for new plants led them to hybridizers Halfdan Lem, Lester Brandt, Endre Ostbo, Hjalmar Larson, and Ben Nelson and to membership in the American Rhododendron Society. They also added hybrids from England and a rich collection of companion plants. After Max died in 1979, Ann continued her interest in rhododendrons and began hybridizing herself. In her will, she left the garden to the Seattle Rhododendron Society (Seattle Chapter) for the purpose of developing a test and display garden. Meerkerk Rhododendron Gardens are maintained by a resident manager and an enthusiastic group of volunteers. Of particular interest is the test garden, designed by Clive Justice of Vancouver, British Columbia. The circular test garden bed is divided into several pie-shaped wedges planted with new hybrid rhododendrons for testing and rating. Each year the plants in one wedge are removed to make room for a new set of plants for testing.

Cecil and Molly Smith of St. Paul, Oregon, began their garden in the early 1950s, out of a love of native and selected exotic plants, especially rhododendrons. The garden of several acres sloping north to the Willamette Valley floor with a canopy of Douglas fir offers protec-

O'Donnell

Hybrid Test Garden, Meerkerk Rhododendron Gardens

Smith

Cecil and Molly Smith

tion for the large-leaf species along with hardier varieties. The Smiths paid careful attention to each plant's needs for sun and shade, water, and protection from cold. Cecil was particularly fond of *Rhododendron degronianum* ssp. *yakushimanum*, using it as a parent to produce his outstanding hybrids 'Noyo Brave' and 'Cinnamon Bear' which flourish in the garden today. In 1984, when the Smiths could no longer care for the garden themselves, the Portland Chapter purchased the garden and along with the Willamette and Tualatin chapters now manage and care for the garden.

In 1982, the Tualatin Chapter began a display garden at the Jenkins Estate in Aloha, Oregon. Ralph and Belle Jenkins built the residence in 1915, surrounding it with a professionally designed garden that required some

Jones

Cecil and Molly Smith Garden

Smith

Jenkins Estate Sign

twenty-five gardeners to maintain it. The estate was purchased by the Tualatin Hills Park and Recreation District, and the Tualatin Chapter, under the leadership of Bob Ross, a chapter member and landscape designer, developed a rhododendron display garden at the site periphery with over 600 species and hybrid rhododendrons. The plantings include rhododendrons from the Tom McGuire and George W. Clarke collections.

On the northern coast of California near Fort Bragg, the Noyo Chapter has been instrumental in developing a collection of rhododendrons suited for that benign climate at the Mendocino Coast Botanical Gardens. The gardens rely on the prodigious effort of volunteers for much of its maintenance. The big-leaf

Smith

Jenkins Estate

species, selections from subsection *Maddenia*, and vireya rhododendrons receive much attention as volunteers find appropriate microclimates where they will thrive. Peter Schick, a volunteer from the Noyo Chapter of the American Rhododendron Society, was awarded the Bronze Medal from the society for his many projects at the gardens.

In 1980, the Southern California Chapter worked with the University of California, Los Angeles, Botanical Garden to develop two sites, one sunny and one shady, to display the vireya rhododendrons, which are so well suited to the frost-free environment of the region. The university prepared the site, and the chapter provided soil amendments and plants. The university also took on the responsibility of watering and fertil-

izing, with the chapter as overseer. Chapter members involved with the project were Bill Paylen, Carl Deul, and Bill Moynier.

On Vancouver Island in Canada, the city of Nanaimo was the recipient of the Ellen Hailey hybrid rhododendron collection in 1975. Captain Alfred Hailey and his wife, Ellen, a founding member of the Vancouver Rhododendron Society, established a rhododendron collection in Vancouver, moved it to their home in Nanaimo in 1967, and later gave many of the species to the city of Vancouver and the hybrids and several species to the city of Nanaimo. However, the Nanaimo collection became overgrown and vandalized. In 1992 the Nanaimo Chapter "adopted" the collection, which is planted in the Hailey Rhododendron Grove in Nanaimo's Bowen

Tod

Comox Valley Rhododendron Garden

Park. Among the named hybrids are 'Etta Burrows', 'Snow Queen', 'Avalanche', and 'Mrs. Charles E. Pearson', but also included are a number of unnamed hybrids and species.

The North Island Chapter on Vancouver Island built a display garden, the Comox Valley Rhododendron Garden, in the city of Courtenay with over 120 varieties of hybrids and species. The chapter worked with the city's Partner in Parks program, creating a display garden in the center of a high pedestrian traffic area. The city provided soil, mulch, irrigation, and gravel for the paths, while the chapter provided plants, plant identification, signs and labor for construction and maintenance.

And in Oakland, California, The California Chapter, under the leadership of Bill Moyles, has built a vireya rhododendron display garden in Oakland.

American Rhododendron Society Files

Dr. J. Harold Clarke

NOMENCLATURE AND REGISTRATION

To "catalog named varieties of rhododendrons; to register names of new rhododendron hybrids"–other goals set forth in the Articles of Incorporation–the society borrowed from the yearbooks of the Rhododendron Association in England the names of hybrids and species in cultivation for its own yearbooks. In subsequent publications, *Rhododendrons* published in 1956 and *Rhododendrons For Your Garden* published in 1961, the society began to add lists pertaining more to species and hybrids grown in America, adding American hybrids as they entered the market. The task was a mighty one.

As taxonomists refined the species classification, "splitting" and "lumping" subgroups as they went along and creating confusion

among gardeners, the society came to rely on the taxonomists at the Royal Botanic Garden, Edinburgh, for classification of species. Therefore, in its journal currently, species names comply with classification as published in *The Genus Rhododendron: Its Classification & Synonymy*, published by the Royal Botanic Garden, Edinburgh, in 1996. Cataloging species in its journal publications is no longer done.

Sorting out the confusion over "fancy" names given to hybrids was no small task either. In 1949, Dr. J. Harold Clarke, as chairman of Committee on Nomenclature and Registration, began to clarify matters. In a report to the society, he distinguished the difference between the hybrid propagated asexually resulting in a clone and a group of hybrid seedlings of a particular cross. The first would be designated by a fancy name and the second by the fancy name followed by "group."

As American hybridizers began producing their own cultivars and naming them, another area of confusion arose. Names were sometimes given that had already been used for other cultivars or the names were not in compliance with the *International Code of Botanical Nomenclature*. In 1971, the society urged that American breeders send their proposed names to the American registrar, the first of whom was Jock Brydon, for approval. In 1973, the new American registrar, Edwin Parker, began the tradition of listing newly registered names of American cultivars in the *Quarterly Bulletin*, a tradition continued to this day under North American Registrar of Plant Names Jay Murray.

From the beginning, the society was adamant about adhering to an accepted horticultural standard regarding classification of rhododendron species and cultivar names, especially in its publications.

Seattle Times Photo

Dr. J. F. Rock admiring a plant of *R.lindleyi* in the University of Washington Arboretum greenhouse. Mr. Brian Mulligan, director, on left.

PLANT AWARDS

By the late 1940s, American hybridizers were busily creating their own hybrids particularly suited to their region. J. Harold Clarke's Committee on Nomenclature and Registration established an award program to "grant recognition to worthy new varieties of rhododendrons and azaleas and to the breeders who have produced them" (ARS Committee on Nomenclature and Registration 1949). The society's Plant Award Program developed from the committee's suggestions. In 1987, the society revised the Plant Awards Program to include three awards: Conditional Award (CA), Award of Excellence (AE), and Superior Plant Award (SPA). In addition, a regional designation indicated the area where the award was significant (ARS 1987).

MORE IDEAS FOR PROMOTING RHODODENDRONS

To achieve the goal of doing "any and all acts or things necessary, convenient or desirable in the promotion and development of the growing and culture of rhododendrons," as stated in the Articles of Incorporation, the society was never at a loss for ideas. In 1948, members of the society privately underwrote a seed collecting expedition by Dr. Joseph Rock. Rock sent sacks of seeds to John Bacher who disseminated them through the society. In 1954, the British plant explorer Frank Kingdon-Ward invited society members to contribute to his expedition to Burma and in return receive seeds he collected.

ARS Journal Photo

C. I. Sersanous, 1883-1958

Berry of Aberdeen, Washington, in charge. She encouraged members to collect seed from their gardens; the first list of contributor included twenty-five. Some worried that the species seed might not be "true" species, but the desire to give members the pleasure of growing rhododendrons overrode this concern. For fifty cents a packet, members could take part in the excitement of growing rhododendrons from seed. Berry chaired the seed exchange for thirteen years, during which time she refined the procedures for seed packaging and corresponded with contributors all over the world. After her long tenure as chairman she took the job of the society's executive secretary for three years.

Another West Coast member, Linda Wylie of Eugene, Oregon, took the chairmanship of the seed exchange in 1989 and, like Berry, fostered its success with careful handling of seed and voluminous correspondence. The seed exchange has

In 1952, the society began awarding individuals with medals for their contribution to the genus. The first Gold Medal was given to C. I. Sersanous.

In 1954, the society started the Slide Library for use by chapters.

In 1956, the society published the book *Rhododendrons 1956*, edited by J. Harold Clarke, which included American hardiness ratings. In 1991, Herb Spady of Salem proposed a revision of the concept of rhododendron hardiness, which was later endorsed by the society (Spady 1991).

Under the society's third president, Dr. J. Harold Clarke, the 1961 International Rhododendron Conference was held, and in 1964, the society started a seed exchange with Esther

Berg

Esther Berry

proved particularly popular with hybridizers, who could save time by growing on others' crosses for their own use.

Under Alfred Martin of Ambler, Pennsylvania, president from 1973 to 1975, the society founded the American Rhododendron Society Research Foundation. Dr. August Kehr, the Eastern Vice-president at the time, organized the endeavor, which was initially funded by the seed exchange. In 1973, the society announced that its first research grant of $1,000 for two years would be given to Dr. W. C. Anderson of Washington State University for the development of tissue culture in the propagation of rhododendrons. Since that time, the foundation has funded rhododendron researchers all over the world.

THE PACIFIC RHODODENDRON SOCIETY

Most West Coast rhododendron enthusiasts found their home in the American Rhododendron Society, but one man, Leonard Frisbie of Puyallup, Washington, rejected the mainstream and formed the Pacific Rhododendron Society, filing papers for incorporation in 1949. He began monthly meetings in Tacoma, Washington, instructing members in the rudiments of botany. Members experimented with propagation, especially of azaleas, and held spring shows. Frisbie also explored the southwest corner of Oregon and northern California, searching for different forms of *Rhododendron occidentale*. He petitioned the Washington State Legislature to change the name of the Washington State flower from *R. californicum* to *R. macrophyllum*. Many members of the Pacific Rhododendron Society were also

members of the American Rhododendron Society, whose momentum finally overshadowed Frisbie's group.

During the 1980s and 1990s, West Coast members of the American Rhododendron Society focused on improved methods of growing the increasing numbers of species and hybrids that had proved they could thrive in the climate. Among the most consuming of interest for many, however, became the creation of their own hybrids. The compelling thrill of hybridizing fired them to create beauties of which the society's founding members could only have dreamed.

Goheen

R. macrophyllum

Greer

R. macrophyllum 'Albion Ridge'

CHAPTER 5

THE HYBRIDIZERS OF OREGON

The creative impulse to hybridize was bound to surface in the rich milieu of rhododendron species and hybrids that had reached the West Coast by the 1940s. To create new rhododendrons even more handsome than their parents excited the imagination of many a grower and, in many cases, compelled them to pursue the dream for the rest of their lives. Mixing genes to create a new and better plant required patience, horticultural skill, and knowledge of the genus. It also required a gambling spirit, which the new hybridizers had in abundance. The result was a whole new array of rhododendrons for the West Coast garden.

THE EARLY HYBRIDIZERS

The earliest well-known Oregon rhododendron hybridizer was James Barto. This pioneer rhododendron grower in Junction City, Oregon, is best known for his species selections of which the most famous is 'Barto Blue', a selection of *Rhododendron augustinii*. Yet Barto also involved himself in hybridizing, making mostly primary crosses of Asian species. 'Barto Alpine', with pink flowers, is a cross of two subsection *Lapponica* species. The fragrant, ivory flowered 'Barto Ivory' resulted from a cross between *R. fortunei* and an unknown plant. The pink flowered and fragrant 'Barto Lavender' probably is a result of *R. fortunei* crossed with *R. ponticum*. 'Esquire', with its long, pointed buds and pink flowers, is a cross of *R. griersonianum* with an unknown plant. 'James Barto', with funnel-shaped pink flowers is probably a cross of *R. orbiculare* with *R. williamsianum*. Barto used two English hybrids to create his

'Renaissance' ('Loderi King George' x 'Peter Koster'). 'Spring Dance', similar to the species *R. triflorum*, is a cross of that species with an unknown plant. Even Barto, whose energies in those early days of rhododendrons on the West Coast were focused on collecting, propagating, and growing on species from Asia, could not keep from dabbing the pollen of one plant onto another. Unfortunately, Barto's records were lost in the house fire, and goals of his hybridizing program are unclear.

Del James, a locomotive engineer, and his wife, Ray, both descendants of Oregon pioneering families, were among the very early rhododendron collectors and hybridizers in Oregon. As early as 1940 they were purchasing rhododendrons from James Barto and John Henny to plant at their home near Hendricks Park in Eugene. They were swept up in the rhododendron enthusiasm and began making contact with others of like mind, finding names in the Royal Horticultural Society literature. One of these was Mrs. Chauncy Craddock of Eureka, California, who sent them a 175-pound plant of *Rhododendron campanulatum*. Others who shared information, plants, and seeds were the curator of Kew Gardens, Halfdan Lem of Seattle, Edmond Amateis

Goheen

'Fawn'

of New York, Mrs. A. C. U. Berry of Portland, Dr. Paul J. Bowman of Fort Bragg, Harold Epstein of New York, Mr. and Mrs. J. B. Stevenson of Towercourt, England, and Edgar Greer of Eugene. The Jameses were charter members of the American Rhododendron Society

In their hybridizing efforts, the Jameses made frequent use of *Rhododendron* 'Fawn' (*R. fortunei* ssp. *fortunei* x Fabia Group), drawing on the orange flowers of *R. dichroanthum* in Fabia Group as other early hybridizers, such as Rudolph Henny, did. One of the results was 'Springfield' ('Umpqua Chief' x 'Fawn') with salmon orange, flat-faced flowers with rolled-back edges and narrow, dark green leaves. This plant is still on the market.

As West Coast hybridizers began producing their own crosses, they began using each other's creations. Halfdan Lem's hybrid 'Anna' ('Norman Gill' x 'The Honourable Jean Marie de Montague') proved to be a breakthrough in the first generation of West Coast hybrids. The parents of 'Anna' are two English hybrids with species parentage traced to *Rhododendron griffithianum* and *R. arboreum*. The flowers of 'Anna' are a dark pink shading to light pink with a red eye, and its foliage begins as bronze changing to dark green.

James

**Jim Russell and Del James, right,
visiting the Sunnydale Nursery in England.**

Greer

'Award'

Del James used 'Anna' to produce 'Award' ('Anna' x 'Margaret Dunn') with white flowers and a yellow flare and 'Half Penny' from the same cross with yellow flowers and red blotch. Both of these hybrids exhibit the bronze new growth of 'Anna'. The parent 'Margaret Dunn' has *R. fortunei* and the Fabia Group, hence *R. dichroanthum*, in its lineage.

Del James also made use of the Rothschild hybrid 'Idealist' (*R. wardii* x 'Naomi') to produce 'Indian Penny' (Sarita Loder Group x 'Idealist') with yellow flowers and 'Ray' (*R. fortunei* x 'Idealist') also with yellow flowers, neither of which is on the market today. However, his hybrid 'Comstock' (Jalisco Group x Jasper Group), with the species *R. fortunei*, *R. campylocarpum*, *R. dichroanthum*, and *R. decorum* in its lineage, is still popular, with its orange streaked with apricot and yellow flowers, large calyxes, and round, bright green leaves. Del James is credited with twenty-seven named crosses and was unquestionably one of the most prolific of the early Oregon hybridizers.

In the early years in Oregon where the rhododendron interest was keen among nurserymen, John Bacher produced two hybrids, registered in 1958, by crossing the English hybrids 'Unknown Warrior' and the Fabia Group. His 'Bacher's Gold' bears salmon pink flowers with yellow centers, and his 'Geneva' bears pink frilled flowers. Species in the parentage include *Rhododendron griffithianum*, *R. dichroanthum*, and *R. griersonianum*. Bacher's hybrid 'Bern', bearing flowers of mauve with light centers, is a cross using *R. decorum* as a parent. These species, all of which bore outstanding flowers, were to play major roles in the West Coast hybridizing efforts.

One of the first crosses of Theodore Van Veen, Sr., was *Rhododendron griersonianum* with 'Countess of Derby'. The English hybrid 'Countess of Derby' ('Pink Pearl' x 'Cynthia') was often used by the early hybridizers. The outstanding 'Van' was the result of Van Veen's cross, bearing dark pink flowers on a hardy, compact plant. Coming out of the same cross was 'Lucky Strike' with salmon pink flowers. Theodore Van Veen hybrids, however, are more often characterized by their warm orange to orange-red flowers, the hues presumably inherited from the species *R. dichroanthum*. Hybridizers sought out *Rhododendron dichroanthum*, a native of China, for its ability to pass on its orange, orange-red, and yellow-red blooms to its progeny. The Fabia Group, which Van Veen used as a parent, is a cross of *R. dichroanthum* and *R. griersonianum*. 'Old Copper' ('Vulcan' x Fabia Group), which owes its species parentage to *R. griersonianum*, *R. dichroanthum*, and *R. griffithianum*, bears late blooming orange flowers. 'Autumn Gold' (*R. fortunei* ssp. *discolor* x Fabia Group) bears salmon orange flowers with a dark orange eye, and coming out of the same cross is 'Maryke' with pink and yellow flowers. Like the Greigs and Bacher, Theodore Van Veen was drawn to the warm flower hues. The Van Veen Nursery also was a leader in introducing new West Coast hybrids to the market, including the extraordinary 'Anna Rose Whitney', a cross by Van Veen, and 'Fred Hamilton', a cross by Halfdan Lem of Seattle.

Greer

'Autumn Gold'

Theodore Van Veen's son, Ted Van Veen, after a 22-year career with IBM, took over the presidency of the Van Veen Nursery in 1961 upon the death of his father and has continued the tradition of offering the best new hybrids to the public. He is the author of numerous articles on rhododendrons and the book *Rhododendrons in America*. He received the American Rhododendron Society Gold Medal in 1976. His daughter, Kathy Van Veen, now is supervisor of operations.

Van Veen

Ted Van Veen and his daughter, Kathy, in the Van Veen Nursery

Besides editing the *Quarterly Bulletin for the American Rhododendron Society*, Rudolph Henny of Brooks, Oregon, was a prolific hybridizer in the early years of rhododendron enthusiasm, producing some seventy-five named hybrids during his twenty-four years of making crosses. His hybridizing goals, as related by Cecil Smith in the *Quarterly Bulletin of the American Rhododendron Society*, were to create plants hardy in the Northwest with distinctive blooms (Smith 1963). He favored campanulate shaped corollas and, if the truss were lax, flowers covering the plant. His goals were to produce red flowers without any blue tinge, and yellow flowers of a uniform daffodil yellow. Besides the desired flowers, the plant should have fine foliage and habit. Henny practiced great discipline and destroyed thousands of seedlings that did not live up to his aims.

Greer

'C.I.S.'

In 1944, Henny made the cross that would produce the highly lauded 'C.I.S.' ('Loder's White' x Fabia Group), named for C. I. Sersanous. In loose trusses it bears orange-yellow flowers changing to creamy apricot with an orange-red throat on an upright plant with twisting leaf tips—distinctive blooms, to be sure, with hardiness of 5°F (-15°C). *Rhododendron dichroanthum* through the Fabia Group undoubtedly influences the flower color of this gem. 'C.I.S.' received the Preliminary Award from the American Rhododendron Society and the Award of Merit from the Wisley Trials.

Also influenced by *Rhododendron dichroanthum* through the Fabia Group were Henny's crosses 'Goldbug' (*R. wardii* x Fabia Group) with flowers of red fading to yellow and maroon speckling, 'Jade' (Fabia Group x 'Corona') with orange, pink, and yellow flowers, 'Little Pudding' (*R. decorum* x Fabia Group) with rose to coral flowers, and 'Little Sheba' (Fabia Group x *R. forrestii* Repens Group), a dwarf with red flowers. His 'Tidbit' (*R. dichroanthum* x *R. wardii*) bears red flowers that turn yellow. His rose-red flowering 'Brickdust' (*R. williamsianum* x 'Dido') carries *R. dichroanthum* through its pollen parent.

Henny produced a number of red flowering hybrids using the species *Rhododendron facetum* which bears bright red flowers on a plant of varying habit, including 'Captain Jack' ('Mars' x *R. facetum*) and 'Cavalier' ('Radiance' x *R. facetum*). The dwarf 'Voodoo' ('Britannia' x 'May Day') has the red flowering *R. haematodes* and *R. griersonianum* buried in its parentage as does his 'Doctor Ross' (*R. griersonianum* x 'Borde Hill') and his 'Captain Kidd' ('Princess Elizabeth' x 'May Day'), with the added *R. thomsonii*.

Henny's well-known 'Lake Labish' ('Lady Bligh' x 'Loderi Venus'), with rose campanulate flowers, has a strong *R. griffithianum* influence in both parents, and 'Leona' ('Corona' x 'Dondis'), with large pink trusses, has the influence of *R. fortunei* and *R. arboreum*.

Rudolph Henny's garden in the Willamette Valley of Oregon was praised by Molly Grothaus in the *Quarterly Bulletin of the American Rhododendron Society*, 1963. Here, on his onion farm, he grew on his many seedlings amid a variety of select rhododendrons and companions in his beautifully designed garden.

Ted Van Veen said of Rudolph Henny: "Rudolph was a gentle person of soft voice, deeply religious, loved nature and flowers, and his life was devoted to serving and giving of himself for the good of others" (Van Veen 1984). He was awarded a Gold Medal posthumously in 1963 by the American Rhododendron Society.

John Henny, whose influence among rhododendron growers was discussed in Chapter 4, also was involved in hybridizing even though he was not as prolific as his brother Rudolph. His star hybrid is 'Cotton Candy' ('Loderi Venus' x 'Marinus Koster') with frilled pink flowers and a red blotch on a tall truss. This hybrid is still on the market.

Goheen

'Cotton Candy'

Another founding member of the American Rhododendron Society, George D. Grace of Portland, also produced several hybrids in the early days of West Coast hybridizing. 'Circus' (Fabia Group x 'Purple Splendour') bears flowers in a complex of colors—pink aging to orange with yellow spots and red margins. 'May Song'

('Bow Bells' x Day Dream Group) also bears flowers of varying color—rich rose changing to pale yellow with a rose eye and fading to white. His 'Mount Mazama' ('Britannia' x Loderi Group) bears fuchsia red flowers spotted with bright red, dark red nectar pouches, and stripes on the reverse.

Nurseryman Robert Bovee of Portland introduced many West Coast hybrids to the gardening public, including many of the Arthur and Maxine Childers hybrids, and was an avid promoter of the genus. He also was a hybridizer—one of the first to use the Japanese species *Rhododendron degronianum* ssp. *yakushimanum* or "yak." The introduction of this rhododendron into the gene pool of West Coast hybrids rocketed hybridizing into a new dimension. Here, it seems, was the plant everyone was waiting for. Its neat, mounding form, its hardiness, its silver and tan indumentum, and its lovely recurved leaves gave hybridizers a topnotch plant form with good foliage texture. They could hardly wait to put colorful blooms on it! Its pink fading to white flowers were lovely, but in the hybridizer's mind left room for improvement.

In 1955, Bovee's cross of *Rhododendron degronianum* ssp. *yakushimanum* 'Koichiro Wada' with 'Bow Bells' ('Corona' x *R. williamsianum*) bloomed for the first time and was named 'Kristin'. The flowers kept the pale pink color of its parent species but with red spotting. The same cross produced his 'Virginia Anderson' with pink flowers fading to white with red stripes. He made the primary cross of 'Koichiro Wada' with *R. wardii* and produced 'Bob Bovee', which took for its flowers the yellow from the *R. wardii*. Crossing 'Kochiro Wada' with Rudolph Henny's 'Jade' he produced 'Kevin', with bright pink flowers shading to yellow-pink and large indumented leaves. A cross of 'Koichiro Wada' with 'Vanessa' resulted in 'Mardi Gras' with large leaves and pink flowers. A cross of the species with the Kiev

Bovees Nursery

The Bovees Nursery continues to offer West Coast hybrids to the public.

Group produced 'New Hope' with large, narrow leaves and dark pink fading to a lighter pink in the flowers.

Robert Bovee was also interested in the Knap Hill azaleas and introduced a number of his own crosses and those of Arthur Childers. Among them were: 'Arctic Sun', 'Balls of Fire', 'Bryon Mayo', 'Cathye Mayo', and 'Chimes'.

During the 1950s, Robert Bovee was a frequent contributor to the *Quarterly Bulletin of the American Rhododendron Society*. The Bovees Nursery continues in business today under Lucie Sorensen Smith, and her husband, E. White Smith, who have expanded its offerings of vireya rhododendrons, including their own crosses and those of Peter Sullivan of San Francisco, Peter Schick of Fort Bragg, California, and William Moynier of Los Angeles.

Dr. Carl Phetteplace of Eugene, also a charter member of the American Rhododendron Society, was introduced to rhododendrons by Del James and John Henny after a disappointing experience growing camellias that frequently succumbed to freezes. His rhododendron collecting and the fellowship of other rhodophiles led him to hybridizing. Still available is his 'Abegail'

C. Smith

Carl Phetteplace

('Loder's White' x *R. calophytum*) with soft pink flowers of good substance and large sturdy leaves. Using James Barto's selection of *Rhododendron augustinii*, 'Barto Blue' and 'Bluebird' he produced the popular 'Crater Lake' bearing bright violet-blue flowers and new bronze growth. He used the yellow flowering 'Crest' to produce 'Gretchen Gossler' ('Idealist' x 'Crest') and 'Queen of

Greer

'Crater Lake'

McKenzie' ('Idealist' x 'Crest'). And he crossed Rudolph Henny's 'C.I.S.' with 'Crest' to produce 'Ted Drake.'

Carl Phetteplace also tried his hand with the species *Rhododendron degronianum* ssp. *yakushimanum*. One of his most successful crosses is 'Aloha' ('Vulcan' x *Rhododendron degronianum* ssp. *yakushimanum* Exbury form), with dark pink flowers and red spotting, fading to purple pink, and with a rounded, dense plant habit. Equally successful is his 'September Song' ('Dido' x 'Fawn'). The species *R. dichroanthum* with its orange flowers is buried in the parentage of both seed and pollen parent. The orange flowers of 'September Song' cover this wide, compact growing plant; its attractive olive green leaves are an added bonus.

Stewart

'September Song'

Arthur Childers of Eugene, a millwright by profession but a rhododendron perfectionist at heart, was drawn into the world of hybridizing when his wife, Maxine, gave him a plant of 'Purple Splendour' for Father's Day in 1950. From that day on this self-taught botanist along with his wife immersed himself in the genus. Although he presented a gruff exterior, those who knew him well found a knowledgeable and giving man. Arthur was meticulous in his research and in pursuing his prime hybridizing goal, the "perfect yellow."

Childers

Arthur Childers

Among the Knap Hill azaleas, he self pollinated 'Cecil' with bright red flowers and a bright
orange-red blotch to produce: 'Arctic Sun' with
white flowers, an orange yellow blotch, and yellow margins; 'Del's Choice' with pink to red flowers and orange blotch; 'One-O-One' with deep
orange flowers and an orange blotch; 'Gladngay'
with orange-yellow flowers and red-orange blotch;
'Torcia' with red flowers with an orange blotch;
'Pom Pom' with orange flowers and red blotch;
and 'Pure Gold' with light orange flowers and
orange blotch.

In his elepidote cross 'Ming Toy' (Medusa
Group x 'Crest'), Childers came close to realiz-
ing his goal of the perfect yellow. It bears deep
yellow flowers with shadings of orange on a broad
plant. Other Childers hybrids in the market today are: 'Tanana' (*R. decorum* x [*R. degronianum*
ssp. *yakushimanum* Exbury form x *R. degronianum*
ssp. *yakushimanum* Exbury form]) with white
flowers, olive green leaves, and compact habit;
'Star Trek' (*R. davidsonianum* x 'Ruth Lyons') with
purple flowers and dark green foliage; and
'Maxine Childers' (*R. strigillosum* x 'Elizabeth')
with bright red flowers, orange-brown
indumentum, and red new growth.

Cecil Smith, a grass seed farmer in St. Paul,
Oregon, became interested in decorative plants
about 1942. Ten years later, in 1952, when he
saw *Rhododendron* 'Pink Pearl' in Rudolph Henny's
garden he was forever hooked on rhododendrons.
Cecil and his wife, Molly, created a garden fea-
turing rhododendrons and entertained visitors
from around the world. The Smiths were active
in the American Rhododendron Society from the
start. Cecil served on its board of directors for
eighteen years and received the society's Gold
Medal in 1967 and the Pioneer Achievement
Award in 1985. He was also a founding member
of the Rhododendron Species Foundation.

Among Cecil Smith's many rhododendron
crosses are several truly landmark plants, revealing a remarkable hybridizer's instinct. Among the
species he used, *Rhododendron degronianum* ssp.
yakushimanum 'Koichiro Wada' ranks high, con-

Greer

'Noyo Chief'

Greer

'Noyo Brave'

holds dark green leaves with gray-brown indumentum on a wide plant. 'Yellow Saucer' (*R. aberconwayi* x ['Koichiro Wada' x Fabia Group]), selfed, is open growing with glossy foliage and yellow and orange flowers.

One of the great early hybrids was produced in 1955 by Olin O. Dobbs of Eugene: 'Olin O. Dobbs' ('Mars' x 'Purple Splendour'), with large dark purple-red flowers of heavy substance in trusses of perfect conical shape.

Arthur O. Wright of Canby, Oregon, began the Wright's Nursery in 1946 and soon became interested in rhododendrons. He and his son, Arthur A. Wright, became involved in hybridizing rhododendrons in the early flush of rhododendron interest. Their first goals were better flower color and bigger trusses with later emphasis on bud set, foliage, and habit. The star of their creations was 'Odee Wright' ('Idealist' x 'Mrs. Betty Robertson'), a compact plant bearing clear yellow flowers. The Wright Nursery also introduced the lovely 'Anah Kruschke' ('Purple Splendour' x *R. ponticum* seedling), a cross by Franz Kruschke of Clackamas, Oregon. This dense plant with shiny foliage and dark purple flowers also proved to be heat tolerant. Their

tributing to the fine plant habit and foliage of many of his hybrids. To create one of his best, 'Noyo Brave' ('Noyo Chief' x 'Koichiro Wada'), he crossed the "yak" species with the cultivar 'Noyo Chief', which originated in England but was raised by West Coast hybridizer Lester Brandt. 'Noyo Brave' bears bright pink flowers and a red blotch on a well-rounded truss. The reverse cross produced 'Noyo Maiden', a compact plant with indumented dark green leaves and white flowers. He used his own 'Noyo Brave' crossed with the low growing, red flowered 'Elizabeth' to produce 'Belva's Joy', a compact plant with red flowers. His hybrid 'Cinnamon Bear' (*R. bureavii* x 'Koichiro Wada') is coveted for its foliage: heavily indumented narrow leaves and white, fury new growth. The white-flowered, orange-blotched 'Molly Smith' ('Koichiro Wada' x 'Mrs. Furnivall')

Van Veen

'Anah Kruschke'

Goheen

'Mist Maiden'

Greer

'Cary Ann'

lepidote cross 'Oceanlake' ('Blue Diamond' x 'Sapphire') was a winner in all aspects—violet-blue flowers, bronze winter foliage, and compact habit.

Among other Wright Nursery introductions still on the market are 'Cary Ann' ('Corona' x 'Vulcan'), 'Cream Crest' (*R. rupicola* var. *chryseum* x 'Cilpinense'), 'Doubloons' (Moonstone Group x 'Carolyn Grace'), 'Honeydew' ('Carolyn Grace' x Moonstone Group), and 'Peeping Tom' (*R. wardii* x 'Mrs. Furnivall').

Arthur O. Wright also produced Mollis azalea hybrids, particularly ones with red flowers of which several are now growing in the Crystal Spring Rhododendron Garden. The Wright Nursery continued to be an active nursery until 1998.

Greer

'Cream Crest'

Saunders

Mr. and Mrs. Edgar Greer

A cross made at Greer Gardens in the 1950s produced the supremely lovely and successful 'Trude Webster' ('Countess of Derby' x 'Countess of Derby'), with its huge, clear pink flowers and its large, slightly twisted foliage and good habit. It won the first Superior Plant Award from the American Rhododendron Society in 1971. 'Countess of Derby' ('Pink Pearl' x 'Cynthia'), however, was not much used again—at least it was not the parent of many named Greer hybrids. 'Kimberly' (*R. williamsianum* x *R. fortunei* ssp. *fortunei*) is still a popular plant, with light pink flowers covering a low-growing plant.

Edgar Greer is remembered as a kind man, always willing to spend as much time with a visitor at the nursery as the visitor cared to spend. Son Harold, with his wife, Nancy, has carried on the nursery business, making Greer Gardens virtually synonymous with rhododendrons.

Although Edgar Greer was living in Colorado selling insurance in the 1940s when the rhododendron interest was first gathering momentum, once he and his wife, Esther, retired to Eugene in 1951 he was drawn into the current of enthusiasm. His new home in Eugene needed landscaping, and a neighbor supplied him with two rhododendrons from James Barto's collection. In his zest he collected seed from a plant of *Rhododendron ponticum* by the Eugene railroad station and grew it on and soon "had enough grafting stock to supply the country" (Van Veen 1984). Then he met Del James, who encouraged him further. With a vacant lot next door, soon Edgar Greer was in the rhododendron business, always on the lookout for something different and trying his luck with hybridizing. He was particularly interested in tracing the parentage of named hybrids—an interest he passed on to his son Harold, who at an early age exhibited an astounding memory for rhododendron lineage.

Greer

'Trude Webster'

THE SECOND GENERATION OF HYBRIDIZERS

Harold Greer took up hybridizing with a passion, producing an astounding number of fine rhododendrons for one person. Since he started at an early age, he has had the time needed for such accomplishments, but his thorough knowledge of the genus accelerated his work.

Several of his most popular hybrids are small plants suitable for the smaller gardens of the increasing number of rhododendron aficionados. 'Kimbeth' ('Kimberly' x 'Elizabeth'), with the species *Rhododendron williamsianum, R. fortunei, R. forrestii,* and *R. griersonianum* buried in its lineage, grows to approximately 3 feet (1 m) in five years. Pink buds in winter open to bright pink flowers covering the plant. Greer used the species *R. racemosum* to produce a num-

Greer

'Hallelujah'

ber of nice, small lepidote hybrids. The small leafed 'Lois' (*R. pemakoense* x *R. racemosum*), a good rock garden plant, has profusely flowering pink blooms. The flowers of 'Pink Fluff' (*R. racemosum* x *R. davidsonianum*) open light pink and turn dark pink when fully open. 'Shooting Star' (*R. hippophaeoides* var. *hippophaeoides* x *R. racemosum*) bears violet-pink flowers.

Using Del James's hybrid 'Comstock' as a parent, Greer produced 'Cream Glory' ('Comstock' x 'Cheyenne'), which has satiny cream flowers with a large calyx and dark green, rounded leaves, and the aptly named 'Everything Nice' ('Comstock' x 'Unique'), which has pink flowers rayed with a lighter pink and a calyx that gives the flowers a star shape. Both of these hybrids offer something different in their flowers and both are compact and attractive in habit.

One of Greer's most distinctive and successful hybrids is 'Hallelujah' ('The Honourable Jean Marie de Montague' x 'Kimberly'). This probable tetraploid has heavy textured leaves of dark green that bend down in the middle and bright rose-red flowers of heavy substance born in tight trusses.

Greer

Harold Greer

Harold Greer has been active in the American Rhododendron Society virtually all his life, serving as its president, contributing articles to its journal, and giving innumerable lectures illustrated with his own photography. He received the Gold Medal from the society in 1989.

By the time Harold Greer was at the peak of his hybridizing, West Coast hybridizers were often using each other's crosses as parents and producing a new generation of hybrid rhododendrons that differed significantly from the previous generation. Their goals of complex color combinations and purity of color in the flowers, good foliage, and attractive plant habit all were beginning to show up in the new rhododendrons finding their way into West Coast gardens.

Robert Ticknor came to hybridizing through his career in horticultural research. After he received his Ph.D. degree from Michigan State University in 1953, he worked in nursery culture research at the Waltham Field Station at the University of Massachusetts. One of his projects was evaluating the hardiness of evergreen azaleas which were supplied by Ed Mezitt of Weston Nurseries, who interested him in hybridizing. During this period, Ticknor made the cross that would produce 'Summer Rose' (*R. maximum* x 'Romany Chai'), a hardy plant with dark pink flowers and red spotting in a ball-shaped truss.

Al Van Veen

Robert Ticknor and J. Harold Clarke

In 1959, Ticknor moved back to Oregon where he had grown up–near Crystal Springs Lake where the Portland Chapter of the American Rhododendron Society, by this time, had built its test garden. He had been introduced to the garden by Ruth Hansen on one of his trips home from Massachusetts. In Oregon he worked at the North Willamette Experiment Station, which was involved in breeding *Rhododendron* and *Pieris*. Hundreds of rhododendron crosses were made, tested for resistance to *Phytophthora cinnamomi*, and then evaluated. One very unusual and stunning cross credited to Ticknor is an azaleodendron, 'Valley Sunrise' (*R. occidentale* x 'Purple Splendour'), with an orange blotch

Greer

'Valley Sunrise'

Greer

'Shamrock'

against a background of violet. Ticknor's prize, however, is the less flamboyant but exquisite 'Shamrock' (*R. keiskei*, dwarf form x *R. hanceanum* Nanum Group). This lepidote cross, made in 1971, is compact and mounding in habit, growing about 1 foot (.3 m) high in five years and bearing chartreuse flowers. 'Shamrock' is a gem for the rock garden and points the way toward a collection of dwarf West Coast hybrids with *R. keiskei* parentage.

At the North Willamette Experiment Station, Ticknor developed a technique for forcing sterile rhododendron hybrids to set seed by tightening a wire around the stem below the leaves of a shoot with a flower bud at the time the bud starts to open.

In one of his numerous articles for the society's *Quarterly Bulletin*, 1980, Ticknor enumerated the responsibilities of the hybridizer: select cultivars tolerant of the local conditions, recognize that compact plants are more popular than leggy ones, distribute one clone only under a name, choose a descriptive name that is easy to spell, grow the cultivar at more than one location, name only plants intended for introduction to the market, and name only superior and distinct plants.

Robert Ticknor has actively participated in the American Rhododendron Society, serving as secretary/treasurer and taking over as president in 1971. He has also been active on the society's Research Committee.

Howard Slonecker, a civil engineer from Milwaukie, Oregon, was raised on the Oregon Coast where the native *Rhododendron macrophyllum* "grew everywhere." His mother nourished his interest in flowers, pointing out the varying colors of the native rhododendron flowers. As a young boy, he and his friends found a unique use for their spent big brown leaves—smoking them like cigars. Another event occurred in his childhood that would have a more lasting effect. On a family outing to the interior of southwest Oregon, he discovered a plant of the native azalea *R. occidentale*. "I then stored in my mind what the plant and particularly the flowers with the yellow flag in each of the upper petals looked like. I think it was then that a seed was planted in my mind and life has been different ever since" (Slonecker, personal communication). He worked at a nursery during his college years while studying forestry engineering and botany during the Depression but still met no one who knew much about the native azalea. Only when he was assigned to a fire lookout in the Siskiyou National Forest did he witness large stands of the plant, fragrant and varying in flower color. When he and his wife moved to Portland, they built a house in Milwaukie and landscaped it with deciduous

Morris

Howard Slonecker and John Henny judging a Eugene Chapter Show with recorder Phil Tillman.

Greer

'Yaquina'

Greer

'Wallowa Red'

and evergreen azaleas, including *R. occidentale* and the elepidotes 'Pink Pearl', 'Alice', 'Cynthia', and 'Britannia'. To learn more about the genus, he read Clement Bowers' book *Rhododendrons and Azaleas*, and a whole new world opened up for him. He joined the American Rhododendron Society and through it discovered the Barto collection, purchasing a small trailer load in 1947 after Barto had died. Since his job took him to Eugene, he spent at least one evening a week for nearly fifteen years with Del and Ray James in rhododendron "bull sessions."

In 1959, Slonecker started hybridizing using the Knap Hill azaleas as parents to create better yellows. The Slonecker Hybrids, as they are called, are named after Northwest Indian tribes and number about eighteen. The crosses he considered most successful were: 'Yachats' ('Hugh Wormald' x 'Marion Merriman'), with bright yellow flowers, bright orange blotch, and large leaves; 'Clackamas' ('Klondyke' x 'Marion Merriman') with bright orange flowers, a red-orange center, and yellow margins; 'Coquille' ('Hugh Wormald' x 'Marion Merriman') with bright yellow flowers and orange blotch; 'Chetco' ('Hugh Wormald' x 'Marion Merriman') with yellow flowers and orange blotch, and orange-red

backside; and 'Yaquina' ('Hugh Wormald' x 'Marion Merriman') with bright yellow flowers and orange blotch.

Howard Slonecker received the American Rhododendron Society Gold Medal in 1969.

George W. Clarke of Portland established a nursery east of the city, specializing in rhododendrons. He was known as a generous, helpful, and amusing man. David Goheen remembers a big sign at his nursery: "A Person Planting a Rhododendron Too Deep will be Reported to the Nearest Authorities!" Clarke was active in the Portland Chapter of the American Rhododendron Society.

By 1960 Clarke was hybridizing, using *Rhododendron degronianum* ssp. *yakushimanum* in many of his crosses. Two are still on the market. 'Taku' ('Tally Ho' x *R. dedgronianum* ssp. *yakushimanum*) has unusually attractive foliage even for a "yak" hybrid, with leaves thick with indumentum. It bears pink flowers that lighten with age. 'Wisp of Glory' parentage is unknown, but probably a "yak" is present, judging from its yak-like foliage. Its flowers are a light purple-pink. Also on the market is 'Yellow Rolls Royce' ('Crest' x 'Odee Wright') with glossy green foliage and wavy-edged flowers with green accents.

Stubbs

Bill Guttormsen

Bill Guttormsen and his wife, Dolores, began the Greenwood Gardens nursery while Bill was in the dry cleaning business. When he found he sold more rhododendrons and azaleas than other plants, he began to specialize and, in 1960, to hybridize evergreen azaleas, producing the Greenwood Group. His goal was to produce compact, well-shaped plants. Favorite parents were 'Helen Close' for plant form and 'Purple Splendor' for orchid colors. For reds he used 'Glamour' and 'Madrigal'. In 1977, Guttormsen wrote: "The important work has already been done for us by such men as Joseph Gable and B. Y. Morrison. By using these plants as a base, and adding new species or new hybrids, particularly from Japan, we could anticipate the development of many new, outstanding and perhaps exotic plants" (Guttormsen 1977).

Guttormsen has named almost 200 crosses. In 1998, Orris Thompson of Tacoma, Washington, evaluated evergreen azaleas for the Puget Sound region. Of the Greenwood Group, he recommended the red-flowering 'Sulin'(['Louise Gable' x 'Ward's Ruby'] x 'James Gable) and 'Blazon' and 'Sherry' of the same cross. Thompson also recommends 'Can Can' ('Louise Gable' x 'Hermione'), 'Cathy Lynn' of the same cross, and 'Pink Cloud' ('Helen Close' x 'Glamour') (Thompson 1998).

Schoolteachers Ivan and Robertha Arneson of Canby, Oregon, started a nursery in the 1940s, beginning with 10,000 prune trees and expanding to a variety of fruit trees, shade and flowering trees, and shrubs, including rhododendrons. In 1950 the Arnesons bought a 24-acre farm near Canby, the same year they bought their first Mollis azaleas—deciduous, tall, upright plants. When they heard a talk by John Henny on Exbury azaleas, they became interested in the Exbury azaleas too, purchasing liners from Henny's nursery and other suppliers. The Arnesons began hybrid-

Arneson

Ivan and Robertha Arneson

Morris

'Arneson Ruby'

izing these groups of deciduous azaleas in the 1950s. On the advice of Henny, at first they crossed only named azaleas, or a named azalea with seedling, but never a seedling with a seedling. "But as their judgment and the quality of their seedlings developed they began to cross seedling with seedling. They made many crosses, and as these came into bloom they carefully evaluated them to determine which were the best crosses. This enabled them to choose the seedlings to use for further hybridizing. The Arnesons state their theory thus: 'Use the best from each generation to get better'" (Jones 1995).

By the 1980s, the Arnesons were making about 100 crosses a year, with goals of developing intense flower color, especially reds. Their 'Robbins Flame' (Mollis hybrid, red x Mollis hybrid, red) is one example of their success in producing such a red. Their Mollis hybrid 'Arneson Gem' ('C. B. van Nes' x Koster's Brilliant Red Group) has orange-red buds opening to yellow-orange. They produced a good white in 'Mount Rainier'.

They also worked with the Exbury azaleas, adding an Ilam hybrid to their program, to come up with better reds. One of these successes was 'Molalla Red' ([('Gibraltar' x 'Favor Major) x (Gibraltar' x 'Favor Major')] x 'Wallowa Red'). The complicated lineage illustrates the multiple generations that often went into an Arneson hybrid. They also produced petaloid doubles with large flowers, such as 'Fluffy' (['Cecil' x 'Pink Delight'] x ['George Reynolds' x 'Klondyke']).

Marshall Lyons of Eugene dreamed of building a garden during the hard years of the Depression, but after working as an electrician and for the Chase Gardens in Eugene finally he and his wife, Ruth, were able to purchase an acre of land on Garden Way in Eugene in 1941 where they began building their dream garden. With Del and Ray James they visited the Barto nursery and became interested in rhododendrons. On one of their visits they discovered a plant of *Rhododendron davidsonianum* and later registered it as 'Ruth Lyons', considered one of the finest selections of this species.

During the 1950s, Lyons began hybridizing, using mostly English hybrids. Two of his hybrids still available are 'Apricot Nectar' (unknown x Jalisco Group), a compact plant with large leaves bearing orange flowers with red edges in a ball-shaped truss, and 'Blue River' ('Van Nes Sensation' x 'Emperor de Maroc') with violet-blue flowers covering the plant and glossy foliage.

Willard and Margaret Thompson of Waldport, Oregon, established a nursery, after Willard survived World War II in an artillery outfit in the major European campaigns and as a "topper" in the logging industry. Although they began their nursery with fruit trees, they were drawn eventually to rhododendrons. They specialized in indumented species as well as carrying the standard hybrids. Willard was known for his ability to graft rhododendrons and was able to offer many species previously unavailable. In the late 1960s and 1970s they began hybridizing. Their named crosses have proved extremely popu-

Greer

Willard and Margaret Thompson

Greer

Roy and Evelyn Thompson

lar. The vigorous 'Creole Bell' ('Vulcan' x 'Harvest Moon') has dark green foliage and blooms of bright pink with overtones of blue that make it glow. 'Ring of Fire' ('Darigold' x 'Idealist'), a breakthrough in color combinations, made a great hit with gardeners with its golden flowers edged with orange-red and its dense foliage and compact habit. 'Sunspot' ('[Darigold' x 'Lacamas Spice'] x [*R. croceum* x *R. wardii*]) forms a compact plant and blooms in large trusses of yellow flow-

ers. Willard and Margaret were known for their warm hospitality towards visitors to the nursery. Currently the Thompson nursery is run by son Roy and his wife, Evelyn.

In the 1960s, James Elliott and his wife, Eleanore, of Knappa, Oregon, began to develop their nursery on the family dairy farm near Astoria. He became interested in rhododendrons in about 1935, visiting the Cranguyma Nursery and the Clarke Nursery in Washington.

Van Veen

'Creole Bell'

Greer

'Ring of Fire'

In about 1960, Ed Parker of Astoria introduced him to the art of making rhododendrons crosses. He went on to make some 500 crosses in the next twenty years. Elliott frequently corresponded with Halfdan Lem, a man he described as "one of the most unforgettable characters that I have ever known" (Elliott, personal communication). Besides enjoying Lem's geniality and colorful antics, Elliott learned much from Lem through letters and visits to his nursery. After Lem's death, he acquired many of Lem's finest hybrids and his latest crosses still in flats. His hybridizing activity intensified, and after thirty-five years in the dairy business, he became a full-time rhododendron grower and hybridizer. Elliott rigorously culled his hybrids and tested the best for a long time. His goal was to create plants with healthy, green foliage and flowers of heavy substance that hold their fresh opening color over a long period of time. He also wanted plants that would bloom at an early age and hold their fine shape on through the years without pruning. He strove for bicolors different from existing ones and plants that could withstand the region's cold winters.

Elliott produced many outstanding hybrids, the most well-known being 'Naselle' ('Big Sam' x 'Lem's Cameo'), a well-shaped, compact plant with dark green foliage and flowers of pink shad-

Nys

**Eleanore and James Elliott with
Viola and Charles McNew**

ing to yellow with orange spotting, named after the town of Naselle, Oregon, where a number of his customers lived. This plant received the Award of Excellence in 1992 from the American Rhododendron Society. 'Big Sam' ('C.I.S.' x unknown) was Elliott's own cross. His 'Amity' (['Grosclaude' x 'Britannia'] x 'Koichiro Wada') is low growing with silver indumentum on earl foliage. The flowers are pink with red spots and a large calyx. 'Dazzler', of unknown parentage, has indeed dazzling flowers of salmon orange. 'Denali' ('Vanessa Pastel' x 'Pink Walloper') has large trusses of pink

Greer

'Naselle'

Goheen

'Swamp Beauty'

flowers and dark green foliage attractive all year. The low growing 'Flirt' ('Britannia' x 'Koichiro Wada') has dark red buds opening to pink. 'Frontier' (Letty Edwards Group x 'Crest') is upright growing yet round in form with pink flowers shading to yellow in the center. 'Ladies Choice' ('Moonstone' x 'Hawk') is another low grower with yellow flowers and red spotting in a lax truss and glossy leaves. 'Pacific Sunset' (['Peach Lady x 'Tally Ho'] x 'Malemute') grows wider that its height, has dark green, narrow leaves and lax trusses of pink, wavy-edged flowers. 'Malemute' was his own cross that he found made a good parent. 'Sunset Bay' ('Odee Wright' x 'Malemute') is a compact grower with bright yellow flowers, pink flower edges, and green throat. 'Swamp Beauty' ('Purple Splendour' x 'Loderi Superlative') has pink flowers with red spots and long leaves that collar the truss.

Elliott is remembered for his dry wit, enthusiasm and energy—lean and fit even in his later years and usually wearing farmers bib overalls and a baseball cap.

Merle Sanders of Roseburg, Oregon, a logger, and his wife, Belva, became interested in rhododendrons in 1980 when they settled on rhododendrons as the plant to use for landscaping their home because the deer would not eat

Greer

'Mrs. Murples Purple'

them. Soon they were drawn to the genus and began hybridizing after they purchased seed from the American Rhododendron Society seed exchange. They have named a number of crosses by Cecil Smith made in the 1980s, grown from seed from the ARS seed exchange. 'Belva's Joy' ('Noyo Brave' x 'Elizabeth') is a compact growing plant with red buds opening to red flowers. 'Raspberry and Custard' ('Scintillation' x [Jalisco Group x *R. degronianum* ssp. *yakushimanum*]) has flowers of custard color changing to raspberry red covering the plant. Out of the same cross came 'Vicki Dianne', similar to 'Scintillation' but with larger trusses and a darker pink. Also from the same cross is 'Eleanor Moody' with white flowers and a maroon blotch on a plant wider than tall. Their own cross, 'Dreamy Cream' ('Honeymoon', open pollinated) opens with lavender pink flowers changing to peach-cream that cover the plant.

Like many of the enthusiasts of the West Coast, the interests of Dr. Forrest Bump of Forest Grove, Oregon, ranged widely: collecting rhododendrons, viewing the genus in the wild, starting a new chapter of the American Rhodo-

Sanders

Merle Sanders

Bump

Dr. Forrest Bump

dendron Society, and hybridizing. His interest began in 1951 when he received a rhododendron as a house-warming gift. When his wife, Rosy, told him he could propagate rhododendrons from cuttings, he entered the world of rhododendrons, treating each plant with the exacting care he extended to his medical patients. First he built a tent for propagating his cuttings. Next he built a greenhouse using scrap lumber. He perfected his methods of rhododendron culture so expertly he was able to take the large-leaf *Rhododendron macabeanum* through the frigid winter of 1956.

Bump's fascination with the genus continued to grow, and in 1979 he joined a group of other members of the American Rhododendron

Society on a trip to Sikkim in the Himalayas, the first group of westerners allowed to tour Sikkim in twenty-two years.

Although Bump's hybrids carry no registered names, they are products of studiously applying knowledge of others such as Halfdan Lem and learning from his own successes and failures. He recommends "selecting varieties like 'Anna' and 'Purple Splendour' to grow your own parent material. 'Purple Splendour' is an old *ponticum* hybrid and its main quality is that it's richly colored. No matter what color you want to get, you have to start with something that is richer in color and with more concentration of pigment, because there tends to be dilution in the hybridizing process" (Victoria Tanner, personal communication).

After spending much of his adult life working in other parts of the country as a college music professor and administrator, Lansing W. Bulgin returned home to Oregon in 1965 to what seemed like an explosion of the spectacular development of rhododendrons in the Northwest. He was particularly impressed by both their beauty and diversity. The contagion and enthusiasm through membership in the American Rhododendron Society stimulated him to further study and experimentation in rhododendron culture.

In 1975 the Bulgins puchased five acres near Sherwood, Oregon, with the intent to develop a rhododendron nursery as a retirement enterprise. Ellanhurst Gardens became the base for subsequent propagation and hybridization.

The endless generosity of time, knowledge and encouragement by many people but especially J. Harold Clarke and Cecil Smith was instrumental to Bulgin's development in the field. His hybridizing was largely condensed into a period of about ten years. In 1990 the nursery was sold, thus effecting a second retirement.

Bulgin

Lansing and Eleanor Bulgin

Bulgin

'Elrose Court'

A partial list of Lansing Bulgin's hybrids include: 'Yaku Fantasia' ('Vulcan' x *R. degronianum* ssp. *yakushimanum*), 'Yaku Royale' ('Vulcan' x *R. degronianum* ssp. *yakushimanum*), 'Elrose Court' ('Vulcan' x 'Sun Devil'), 'Bold Adventure' ('Ruby Bowman' x 'Skipper'), 'Maui Sunset' ('Old Copper' x 'Skipper'), 'Ellenhurst' ('Purple Lace' x 'Van Nes Sensation').

By the 1990s, the Oregon hybridizers had added a rich, new layer to the West Coast rhododendron phenomenon, building new creations from species, English hybrids, and finally their own hybrids with breakthroughs in foliage, form, and flowers. Interaction with other West Coast hybridizers, especially those from Washington, expanded their horticultural horizons and gave the home gardener a wealth of new plants from which to choose.

Along the way Bulgin served a term as President of the ARS Portland Chapter, and authored the book entitled *Rhododendron Hybrids, A Compendium by Parent*, published in 1986.

CHAPTER 6

THE HYBRIDIZERS OF WASHINGTON

THE EARLY HYBRIDIZERS

Rhododendron hybridizing in Washington grew in intensity once the early hybridizers of the 1940s and 1950s met each other and began exchanging ideas as they gathered in each others' gardens and around each others' dining room tables. These men—for they were mostly men—more often than not came from non-horticultural careers and were self-taught botanists, driven by a desire to learn. Several had additional interest in the arts or other sciences, and everyone, at least to some degree, relished the practice of teaching what he knew to the truly interested beginner. And so a second generation of Washington hybridizers naturally followed the first, building on what it learned from the "masters" to create even better plants.

Many of the early hybridizers lived long lives, and their work overlapped the second generation, which in turn overlaps the current generation. A

progression, however, can be seen as one individual learned from another and one generation learned from the preceding one.

During his nearly thirty years of hybridizing, Halfdan Lem of Seattle, a self-taught student of the genus *Rhododendron*, acquired an exhaustive knowledge of these plants, made numerous breakthroughs with his hybrids, and created a legend among rhododendron growers with his colorful, rambunctious style. This big Norwegian from Ketchikan, Alaska, infused the Northwest rhododendron community with much merriment through his antics as he went about his serious business of creating stupendous new hybrids.

Gwen Bell of Seattle, who knew Lem, has researched his life and work. Halfdan Lem was born in Nordfjord, Norway, and raised in a well-to-do family of twelve children. His love of plants stemmed from his mother, a proficient gardener who collected rare plants. As a young man with a

Van Veen

Halfdan Lem

keen interest in birds and other wildlife, he im-migrated to Ketchikan where he was a fisherman and partner in a fish processing plant. Then, in 1925, a friend gave him a book about rhododen-drons. The accounts of the plant hunters and the beautiful, exotic plants they found changed the course of Lem's life. He began raising rhododen-dron seedlings on his fishing boats. He joined the Rhododendron Society of England and be-gan corresponding with British enthusiasts, among them Fred J. Rose of Stonehill Gardens in Southhampton who sent him seed and whom he later visited. In fact, Lem credits his hybridiz-ing success to the "good stuff" he used as par-ents. In 1933, Halfdan and his wife, Anna, moved to Seattle to start a rhododendron nursery. In Seattle, Lem soon became acquainted with local rhododendron growers and gave them seed from Fred Rose. The gregarious Lem was at the center of an informal group called the Rum Dum Club, which met at each other's houses around a table "piled with good food by their assembled wives, debating vigorously and vividly the merits of cer-tain crosses, rhododendron parents to be used, and the rewards which might result" (Gwen Bell,

personal communication). Among the group were Endre Ostbo, Ben Nelson, Hjalmar Larson, Ernest Anderson, Don McClure, William Whitney, Karl Sifferman, and Harry Madison. Frank Mossman of Vancouver, Washington, who collected and grew on many of Lem's hybrids, remembers Lem as a great entertainer. "He loved to eat and drink. Once I sat with him until 2:30 a.m. drinking and eating some of his famous blood cheese, Blutcaesa, on flatbrot . . . Anna was always a fine entertainer also. We had fre-quent dinners, and she always spread a very beau-tiful table. The cuisine was excellent" (Mossman, personal communication).

By the early 1940s, Lem's collection of rhododendrons and its gene pool were large enough for him to begin a program of hybridiz-ing. Fred Rose's seeds and scions that were sent to Lem to save them from destruction while En-gland was engaged in war played a major part. Lem's enthusiasm was related to Gwen Bell through Mrs. Carl English, who remarked "[Lem] crosses everything with rhododendrons except the chickens." Another account tells of Lem "rush-ing down the paths with pollen on all fingers pollenizing every bloom in sight." Lem kept records of his some two thousand crosses. In any one year he might have 50,000 seedlings lined out.

Impatient for his crosses to bloom, Lem developed a technique of top-grafting in which he grafted 1- and 2-year-old seedlings on older rhododendrons. "It was a fantastic sight to see a 4-foot-tall rhododendron supporting as many as thirty different flowered trusses," Bell recalls. However, with this method he could evaluate crosses sooner because several generations could be raised more quickly.

Bell recalls one of Lem's experiences selling grafted plants to a wealthy Beverly Hills, Califor-nia, customer who ordered a large number of rhododendrons. Because Lem did not like to be away from his plants at home, he did not go to California to supervise the project. Two years later, however, he visited the customer and saw the big house and the spacious lawn ringed by rhododendrons "all blooming bluish ponticum colors." Although Lem offered to prune the shrubs back to the desired hybrids, the owner rejected the offer because he thought these ponticums were the most beautiful flowers on their property.

Bell also recalls that Lem could be outraged at visitors' behavior in his nursery. One day a woman brought her two children to the nursery. While she and Lem searched out a plant, the children removed every label from plants in a cold frame. The result was a new sign at the nursery: No Children Allowed In Nursery.

Lem also liked to play tricks on his friends "He would substitute a different rhododendron for the one requested. Lem would chuckle over the joke for a week, picturing his friend's surprised face when the plant bloomed" (Bell, personal communication). Anna Lem told Bell that her husband always substituted a rhododendron which in his opinion was better than the one the friend thought he had bought. He also could be generous, adding unnamed seedlings along with a purchased plant. After Lem died, in 1969, Anna Lem said to Bell, "He surprised me until the day he died."

Goheen

'Pink Walloper'

"Lem loved big flowers and big plants, showy, tall-trussed reds, rich creams, and of course he hybridized to create big flowered new yellows using pollen from his good bright, yellow-flowered *Rhododendron lacteum*" (Bell, personal communication). His hybrid 'Anna' ('Norman Gill' x 'The Honourable Jean Marie de Montague') with its bronze new growth, long narrow leaves, and ruffled pink flowers with a red eye proved to be an outstanding parent for a number of his subsequent crosses, although other hybridizers had trouble obtaining pollen from it. Lem received the seed that produced 'Anna' from Fred Rose. Besides its attractiveness, 'Anna' passed on its fine attributes to its progeny. Using 'Anna' as the seed parent, Lem crossed it with 'Marinus Koster' to produce the Walloper Group—aptly named for their huge trusses and some fifteen pink, ruffled flowers per truss on a large hardy plant with leathery foliage. Selections from the group are 'Lem's Monarch', 'Point Defiance', 'Pink Walloper', and 'Gwen Bell.' All these large, stunning plants are still on the market. The beautiful 'Isabel Pierce' ('Anna' x 'Lem's Goal') also bears large trusses of ruffled, dark pink flowers with dark flares in the throat and narrow, dark green, glossy leaves.

Van Veen

'Point Defiance'

Van Veen

'Gwen Bell'

Lem's favorite creation—and a favorite parent for many hybridizers—is 'Lem's Cameo' (Dido Group x 'Anna'), named by Anna Lem. This plant offers an ongoing show beginning with leaves that unfold in maroon-red. Round flower buds then open in large upright trusses of some twenty apricot-pink flowers with a red eye in the throat. 'Lem's Cameo', considered a breakthrough when it was introduced in 1963, was the second rhododendron to receive the Superior Plant Award, in 1971, from the American Rhododendron Society.

A "big red" was achieved in 'Halfdan Lem' ('The Honourable Jean Marie de Montague' x 'Red Loderi'), a robust plant with flowers of bright red and foliage of heavy texture. Another "big red" is 'Red Olympia' ('Anna' x 'Fusilier').

Lem also produced a number of hybrids with yellow or yellow-orange flowers. 'Seattle Gold' ('Diva' x 'Lady Bessborough') has colored petioles with warm yellow flowers. The cross (*R. bureavii* x Fabia Group) produced 'Hansel' with tan indumentum and salmon-orange flowers in lax trusses and 'Gretsel', also with tan indumentum but pink flowers edged in salmon-orange. Again using the Fabia Group as a parent, he produced 'Hello Dolly' (Fabia Group x *R. smirnowii*), a hardy, rounded, indumented plant with yellow, orange, and pink flowers named after one of his favorite songs; 'Oz' ('Catawbiense Album' x Fabia Group), a dense plant with yellow flowers, orange spots and pink edges; the hardy 'Wizard' ('Catawbiense Album' x Fabia Group), an apricot and yellow bicolor with streaks of yellow from the throat; and 'Jingle Bells' (Fabia Group x 'Ole Olson'), a dense, low growing plant with flowers opening in red and changing to yellow.

Lem's Norwegian accent was a delight to visitors and friends. Gwen Bell recalls, "My first purchase was a low-growing plant of 'Jingle Bells'. I would have bought that rhododendron just to hear him say 'Yingle Bells.'" He also had his own vocabulary: calyxes became "tudulus," favorite hybrids—or lutefisk—became "fine stuff," and having a problem with rooting became "go stuck." A snort of whiskey became "snurt"—and might be offered to visitors as they toured the garden.

G. Bell

Anna Lem

Endre Ostbo

His naming of plants also became a legend. A man came to the Lem nursery each year to purchase rhododendrons. When the bill was totaled, he would say, "I will have to peel lots of potatoes to pay for this." When a yellow-flowered *R. caucasicum* hybrid bloomed for the first time, the Lems named it 'Potato Peeler' (Bell, personal communication). One of his hybrids named after the king of Norway, 'King Olav V', was presented to the king in Seattle and installed in Norway's Royal Gardens. 'Anna' was, of course, named after his wife, a surprise to her. When a visitor was praising a plant of 'Diane', Lem said, "'Diane' is nice but you should see my 'Anna'." Anna Lem did not know whether he was planning to name this new cross 'Anna' or "if it just came off the top of his head." Lem, however, did not like his own name attached to the hybrid name.

In a personal letter to James Elliott of Knapa, Oregon—for Lem was also an avid letter writer—he wrote in 1966: "It is now midnight and I have to start on my usual walk in the woods for to move the sprinklers for the night. My wife and our two cats follow in case I should fall over and go to the everlasting sleep beneath the good old fir trees" (Elliott, personal communication).

Halfdan Lem received the Gold Medal from the American Rhododendron Society in 1963, three years before he died.

Halfdan Lem's close friend, the shy Endre Ostbo of Bellevue, Washington, also was born in Norway. He came to the United States in 1912, homesteaded in Montana, moved to Everett, Washington, after World War I to work in the Weyerhaeuser mill, and then moved to Medina, Washington, to work as an estate gardener where he became interested in rhododendrons. Ostbo started his own nursery in 1937 in a peat bog near Bellevue. A charter member of the American Rhododendron Society, he was an early, highly literate advocate of the rhododendron's place in the Northwest garden for adding zest to the usual drab collection of cypress, junipers, and camellias. In the

'Martha Isaacson'

society's first publications, he instructed members on imported hybrids suitable for the Northwest and how to place them in the woodland garden. One of the persons who supplied him with seed for hybridizing was Donald Graham of Seattle, who began importing from abroad in 1932. Graham wrote that Ostbo's hybridizing goals were a late blooming rhododendron with flowers of substance and clear color and low growing rhododendrons suitable for the rambling-style houses of the time.

One of Ostbo's most well-known introductions is 'Mrs. Donald Graham' (['Corona x *R. griersonianum*] x 'Loderi'), grown from seed from Fred Rose of England, presumably obtained through Halfdan Lem. Its flowers are a bright salmon-pink on a large open and upright growing plant. Ostbo used this plant to produce 'Jane Rogers' ('Mrs. Donald Graham' x 'Mrs. R. S. Holford'), with pink flowers and a burgundy flare. He also used it to produce his late-flowering 'Lily' ([*R. auriculatum* x 'Alice'] x 'Mrs. Donald Graham') bearing white flowers.

Two unusual crosses of 'Mrs. Donald Graham' with the azalea *R. occidentale* produced the azaleodendrons 'Martha Isaacson'

Van Veen

'Edward Dunn'

with fragrant pink striped flowers and maroon leaves and 'Mary Harmon' also with fragrant, pink-striped flowers.

One of his earliest crosses produced the Olympic Lady Group ('Loderi King George' x *R. williamsianum*), a well-shaped, compact plant with white flowers. Ostbo's most well-known cross, however, is 'King of Shrubs' (*R. fortunei* ssp. *discolor* x Fabia Group) with orange flowers and yellow stripes and attractive narrow leaves on a plant that grows to about 4 feet (1.2 m) in ten years. His late flowering 'Edward Dunn' ([*R. neriiflorum* x *R. dichroanthum*] x *R. fortunei* ssp. *discolor*) also bears orange-yellow flowers. The parentage of 'Ostbo's Low Yellow' is unknown but possibly is a Fabia Group hybrid. This low-growing plant bears flowers in cream, apricot, and yellow that change in color as they mature.

In 1957 Endre Ostbo was awarded the Gold Medal from the American Rhododendron Society. Endre Ostbo's long list of admirable hybrids and his active involvement in the rhododendron community accelerated the rhododendron to its place as "king of shrubs" among Northwest gardeners.

When the studious and sometimes gruff Lester Brandt of Tacoma, Washington, became interested in rhododendrons in 1938, he arranged with one of the largest bookstores in England to send him every book on rhododendrons it had. Like many of the other early growers and hybridizers, he studied the genus assiduously, communicated with English growers, and sent for their seed. Brandt, who was proficient in five languages, was apparently unusually knowledgeable about rhododendrons, even compared to his well-versed contemporaries. At one time he was reputed to have the largest library of rhododendron books in the United States. He joined the Royal Horticultural Society and the Seattle Rhododendron

G. Bell

Lester Brandt

Brandt, of course, associated with other rhododendron growers and hybridizers of the region, although he was known to be somewhat of a loner and irascible at times. In one instance, Brandt stood at the gate as a garden club arrived at his nursery. One of the women reached over the fence and picked a rhododendron flower. Brandt immediately closed the gate and told the group to go home.

On another occasion, he went to Halfdan Lem's nursery to make some crosses on Lem's plants. As he was browsing the nursery he saw Lem do something with one of the flowers he had pollinated and was certain he was tampering with the cross. Brandt was livid and swore he would never go near the nursery again. It may be, however, that Lem was dabbing a bit of his "snoose" on the pistil to help the pollen down the tube. Brandt also had run-ins with Carl Fawcett, who on one occasion disqualified one of Brandt's truss show entries because it had been taken into the greenhouse to avoid freezing.

Two years before he died, Brandt was beaten and robbed at his home—although the robbers left his valuable collection of Samuri swords—"and he never did overcome his fear and distrust of mankind in general" (Hacanson, personal communication).

Society before the American Rhododendron Society was formed, becoming a charter member of the latter when it was founded and serving as an officer in a variety of positions.

Brandt's nursery, on a rocky site east of Tacoma where he lived alone in a cottage, contained many English hybrids, many of which he used in his hybridizing program. He was a consultant for many large estates in Seattle and Tacoma, supplying fine specimens to the owners. His collection included large specimens of the Loderi Group and Naomi Group. A stunning plant of 'Loderi King George' was 15 feet (4.5 m) high and 18 feet (5.5 m) wide. Brandt also supplied the Washington Park Arboretum with rhododendrons, many of them his own hybrids.

Greer

'Fireman Jeff'

Lester Brandt began his hybridizing program to create small, compact plants suitable for modern homes. He used the cross (*Rhododendron forrestii* ssp. *forrestii* Repens Group x Mandalay Group) for the compact red flowering 'Blood Ruby' and 'Little Joe'. And he used the cross (*Rhododendron forrestii* ssp. *forrestii* Repens Group, pink form x 'Bow Bells') for his 'Rêve Rose' and the highly successful 'Lori Eichelser' with its pink bell-like flowers, round bright green leaves, and tight habit. His hybrid 'Thor' (*R. haematodes* x Felis Group) is another low growing plant with red flowers. Bearing flowers of bright red along with a red calyx is the still popular 'Fireman Jeff' ('The Honourable Jean Marie de Montague' x 'Grosclaude'), which grows to approximately 3 feet (1 m) in ten years. The pollen parent has the red flowering *R. haematodes* and *R. facetum* as parents. Perhaps his most popular hybrid to day, however, is 'Kubla Khan' ('Britannia' x 'Goldsworth Orange') with its striking combination of flower colors—pink, orange, red, and

Goheen

'Oliver Twist'

cream with a red flare and large calyx. This is a larger plant, growing to about 5 feet (1.5 m) in ten years.

Brandt kept a record of his hundreds of crosses in code logged in journals.

Ben Lancaster of Camas, Washington, a carpenter by trade, became interested in rhododendrons after he moved from his home in Michigan to Camas. In 1937 while recovering from an automobile accident he read the book *Rhododendrons and Azaleas* by Clement Bowers and came down with a case of "rhododendronitis," as he called it. For the next thirty-three years of his life, this talented man, who also loved music and poetry, devoted himself to rhododendrons. Although the accident left him with crippled legs, he and his wife, Rose, established Lackamas Gardens in 1946, where "instead of a cane he used a shovel" (Goheen, personal communication).

Lancaster was a charter member of the American Rhododendron Society and a recipient of its Gold Medal.

In 1967, Lancaster discussed his hybridizing program in the *Quarterly Bulletin of the American Rhododendron Society*. One of his first discoveries was that hybrids of known parentage often make better parents than the species,

Goheen

Ben and Rose Lancaster

Van Veen

'Yaku Sunrise'

taking advantage of the many years spent by others in selective breeding. He also advises hybridizers to plan objectives rather than using the "shotgun method."

With heat and sun tolerance in mind, along with hardiness, Lancaster used *Rhododendron williamsianum* to produce a dwarf group of hybrids he called the Bell Series. Among the results were: 'Easter Bells' (*R. williamsianum* x China Group) with pink flowers, 'Ivory Bells' ('Chlorops' x *R williamsianum*) with light yellow flowers, 'Mission Bells' (*R. williamsianum* x *R. orbiculare*) with pink flowers, and 'Vulcan's Bells' ('Vulcan's Flame' x *R. williamsianum*) with red flowers.

Lancaster found the then newly introduced 'Koichiro Wada' form of *Rhododendron degronianum* ssp. *yakushimanum* to be an excellent parent for imparting good form and foliage, cold and heat tolerance, and rooting ability. "The one thing of which you can be reasonably sure is this: whatever the size or ungainly proportions of the plant with which you cross *R. yakushimanum*, the progeny will be reduced to garden size in sturdy, many-branched dwarfish to moderate growers," Lancaster wrote. He used 'Koichiro Wada' to create 'Yaku Cream' ('Lackamas Cream' x 'Koichiro Wada'), 'Yaku

Frills' (*R. smirnowii* x 'Koichiro Wada'), 'Yaku Picotee' ('Moser's Maroon' x 'Koichiro Wada'), and the lovely 'Yaku Sunrise' ('Vulcan's Flame' x 'Koichiro Wada') with pink flowers showing dark pink of the reverse and edges.

Ben Lancaster also searched for better yellow flowers in his crosses. 'Lackamas Gold' ('Chlorops' x *R. wardii*) bears bright yellow flowers on a compact plant. 'Aztec Gold' (Indiana Group x 'Inca Gold') has the added attribute of bronze new foliage.

One of his successful primary crosses produced the early blooming 'Snow Lady' (*R. leucaspis* x *R. ciliatum*), white in flower with fuzzy leaves on a dwarf plant. His 'Lackamas Blue' is a *Rhododendron augustinii* selection

Lancaster was also willing to share his negative experience with certain rhododendrons. *Rhododendron griersonianum* passes on its red flowers but along with them a poor plant habit, he wrote. He also stressed the importance of making reverse crosses, noting that seedlings generally inherit plant form and growth habit from the seed parent. Lancaster's wide-ranging hybridizing program included the goals of creating a new group of large-leaf hybrids using *R. macabeanum*, adding fragrance through *R. occidentale*, and producing late bloomers.

Lancaster recognized the benefits of working closely with other hybridizers: "The constant swapping back and forth of pollen, seeds, and small seedlings has promoted a comradeship unequaled in any avocation" (Lancaster 1967).

Hjalmar Larson of Tacoma, a onetime sawmill worker, contributed mightily to the "comradeship" of which Ben Lancaster wrote, as he collected species and hybrids and created his own wonders at his nursery in Tacoma. As early as 1920 he became interested in rhododendrons, urged on by an uncle from Sweden who immigrated to Tacoma. Larson, like so many of the early growers and hybridizers, made con-

G. Bell

Hjalmar Larson

tacts throughout the world for information, seeds, and plants. Among his many contacts were Dr. T. Rokujo of Japan and K. C. Pradhan of Sikkim. At the same time, he helped create the local Washington milieu of rhododendron enthusiasts so important to hybridizers.

Larson began hybridizing in the 1930s and, continuing until his death in 1983, created some fifty named hybrids. Although a number of them are no longer on the market, some are milestones and continue in popularity. A plant of *Rhododendron strigillosum* at the Larson nursery, purchased from Ted and Mary Greig of Vancouver Island, produced a number of red flowering rhododendrons when it was crossed with various hybrids: 'Bert Larson' (Diva Group x *R. strigillosum*),

'Double Winner' (*R. strigillosum* x unknown), 'Malahat' ('Gill's Triumph' x *R. strigillosum*), and 'Etta Burrows' ('Fusilier' x *R. strigillosum*). (Larson named many of his crosses after local, well-to-do women.) Dr. Frank Mossman remembers the specimen of *R. strigillosum* well, for it was a parent for his well-known 'Taurus' (Mossman, personal communication).

Larson, along with his contemporaries, was in pursuit of rhododendron flowers in warm colors. He used the spreading, orange flowering Jasper Group often in his crosses: 'Janet Scroggs' ('Virginia Scott' x Jasper Group); 'Jennifer Marshal' (Jasper Group x 'Alice Franklin'); 'Jo Ann Newsome' (Jasper Group x Dido Group); and 'Bergie Larson' (*R. wardii* x Jasper Group) named after Hjalmar's wife.

One of Larson's most well-known hybrids, 'Mrs. Lammot Copeland' (*R. wardii* x 'Virginia Scott'), bears clear yellow flowers on a large plant with large leaves. Larson crossed 'Mrs. Lammot Copeland' with an unknown yellow hybrid to produce 'Pacific Gold' with red flower buds and yellow flowers and with his own hybrid 'Mary Drennen' to produce 'Spun Gold', with yellow flowers and red spotting. This hybrid was later crossed with *R. degronianum* ssp. *yakushimanum* to produce the lower, more compact 'Orange Marmalade' with red flower buds opening

Greer

'Etta Burrows'

to orange flowers, 'Golden Wedding' with red flower buds opening to yellow flowers, and 'Yellow Pippin' with yellow flowers.

The good influence of *R. degronianum* ssp. *yakushimanum*, which came to the West Coast in the 1950s, shows up in many of Larson's most successful non-yellow hybrids too. 'Pink Sherbet' (*R. degronianum* ssp. *yakushimanum* Exbury form x unknown), a low growing, rounded, dense plant bears pink flowers that fade to white. 'Senator Henry Jackson' (*R. degronianum* ssp. *yakushimanum* x 'Mrs. Horace Fogg') bears pure white flowers on a compact plant with dark green, indumented foliage. 'Skookum' ([*R. degronianum* ssp. *yakushimanum* x 'Mars'] x 'America') exhibits the "yak" form and foliage and bears red flowers with white filaments.

Hjalmar Larson's many years of making crosses span a period in which West Coast hybridizing made great leaps in creating rhododendrons suited to the benign climate and the tastes of a growing number of gardeners. Hjalmar Larson received the Gold Medal from the American Rhododendron Society in 1979 for his part in boosting the rhododendron to its favored place among gardeners.

William Whitney—like Lem, Ostbo, Brandt, Lancaster, and Larson—was a self-taught hybridizer and nurseryman with no formal horticultural training. Born in 1894 near Mount Vernon, Washington, he was an electrician by trade in Washougal, Washington, where he and his wife, Faye, had begun a small nursery with an initial interest in camellias. In 1931, on a business trip to Seattle they stopped at the Malmo Nursery and bought thirty rhododendrons to landscape their home. By 1936, Whitney was fully caught up in rhododendron hybridizing. He met Ben Lancaster, who lived nearby in Camas, and Theodore Van Veen, Sr., of Portland, drawing on their experience to develop his own nursery and hybridizing program. He was a member of the

G. Bell

William "Bill"   Whitney

Rum Dum Club, adding his own high energy to its lively discussions. At an early age, Bill Whitney had stepped into the West Coast's growing rhododendron community—a fellowship of constant give-and-take on one subject: rhododendrons. By 1955, the Whitneys moved their nursery to Hood Canal at Brinnon, Washington, with a much larger site. After Whitney's death, George and Ann Sather took over the ownership.

Whitney's first goal as a hybridizer was to produce offspring superior to both parents in form, foliage, and bloom. His later goals included plants that would root readily, be hardy, thrive in sun, and sustain a low, compact form. During about thirty-five years of hybridizing he raised five generations of blooming plants, combining "the genetic tendencies of many complex clones in a search for plants which are truly outstanding in foliage as well as flower" (Cummins 1965). Working by the principle of mixing all the available genes of plants that could lead to a particular goal, he avoided primary crosses since

Greer

'Anna Rose Whitney'

Stewart

'Virginia Richards'

using existing hybrids saved time. For instance, in his quest for a better yellow, he used the clone (Fabia Group x 'Mrs. Furnivall') crossed with 'Damaris' or 'Crest', drawing on the yellow flowers of *Rhododendron dichroanthum* in the Fabia Group and the form and foliage of 'Mrs. Furnivall' and adding the yellow flower genes of 'Damaris' and 'Crest'.

His technique involved sowing seed in February, transplanting about sixty-five seedlings of each cross to a flat in an open lath bed where they spend two years, and moving them into beds the next year. He then selected about forty of them based on foliage. When the plants were four or five years old, he transplanted them into the open. At six years, when they bloomed, he culled them further. The promising plants were bloomed for three years before evaluation. The whole procedure took eight or nine years. One problem that arose was that he sometimes sold seedlings before they were fully evaluated and named, resulting in confusion over names and lineage of plants in customers' gardens.

'Anna Rose Whitney' (*R. griersonianum* x 'Countess of Derby'), a cross by Theodore Van Veen is named after Whitney's mother. (A sister seedling from the Van Veen cross was 'Lucky Strike'.) The large, well-shaped 'Anna Rose

Whitney' has big leaves and big trusses of pink flowers. The well-known 'Virginia Richards' ([*R. wardii* x 'F.C. Puddle'] x 'Mrs. Betty Robertson'), which illustrates the complexity of some of his crosses, is a smaller, compact plant bearing flowers that open pink and turn to yellow. 'Little Gem' (Carmen Group x *R. elliottii*), which grows to only 18 inches (45 cm), has dark red flowers and glossy leaves, an excellent plant for the rock garden. To produce his 'Hurricane' ('Mrs. Furnivall' x 'Anna Rose Whitney') he used the cross 'Anna Rose Whitney'. Like its pollen parent, it is a vigorous grower with pink flowers marked with dark pink. 'Honeymoon' ([*R. wardii* x 'Devonshire Cream'] x *R. wardii*) is compact with yellow flowers and orange blotch in a green throat.

After purchasing the nursery in 1970, George and Anne Sather introduced many of Whitney's hybrids growing at the nursery, many of unknown parentage. Among these are 'Top Banana' bearing pure yellow flowers on a low plant; 'Anne's Delight', a low growing plant with dark green leaves and yellow flowers; 'Beautiful Dreamer' with yellow flowers and orange markings; 'Joy Ride' with pink flowers and an orange blotch; 'Polynesian Sunset' with flowers in warm colors of orange, peach, and apricot; and 'Whitney's Orange', a low grower with curling leaves and dark orange flowers.

Whitney was reluctant to name a hybrid until he had thoroughly tested it to be sure it attained his high standards. His many beautiful crosses are witness to his diligent efforts and high principles. Bill Whitney received the Gold Medal from the American Rhododendron Society posthumously in 1975.

Ben Nelson, an attorney by profession, owned a nursery on Bainbridge Island, Washington, where he, with his wife Josie, became involved in hybridizing. Dr. Frank Mossman remembers Nelson's many fine plants—fine selections of *Rhododendron vaseyi*, *R. thomsonii*, and *R. roxieanum* var. *oreonastes*—and his generosity in sharing them.

The hybrid rhododendron for which Ben Nelson is best remembered is 'Hotei' ('Goldsworth Orange' x [*R. souliei* x *R. wardii*]) with its bright yellow flowers in a ball-shaped truss. Karl Sifferman may have made the cross, but both men are the documented introducers. Among Nelson's hybrids still on the market are: 'Black Prince's Ruby' (*R. sanguineum* var. *R. haemaleum*), a low grower with red flowers and black veins; 'Klassy's Pride' ([*R. neriiflorum* x *R. strigillosum*] x [Loderi Group x *R. thomsonii*])

Berg

Ben Nelson

with red flowers spotted black; and 'Shirley Rose Lent' (*R. strigillosum* x *R. praevernum*) with dark pink flowers and dark spots.

In a memorial in the *Quarterly Bulletin of the American Rhododendron Society*, Ben Nelson's friend and neighbor Herbert Ihrig wrote: "But great as was his knowledge in this field of horticulture it was Ben the man, the friend, the scholarly gentleman whom we cherished most. He could quote history, poetry and anecdote

Greer

'Hotei'

Goheen

'Ben Nelson Late Red'

with the most learned and yet was unpretentious, straightforward, considerate and kindly to the uninformed" (Ihrig 1970). The American Rhododendron Society awarded Nelson the Gold Medal in 1966. Ihrig himself made several F_2 crosses of the Loderi Group. These large, fragrant shrubs still grow in the Washington Park Arboretum (Mossman, personal communication).

Dr. Rollin Wyrens, a Seattle physician, became interested in rhododendrons when he moved to Washington from the Midwest in 1943 and sought out three of the area's most knowledgeable hybridizers: Halfdan Lem, Endre Ostbo, and Lester Brandt. By 1953, after ten years of collecting, propagating, and visiting rhododendron gardens in England and Scotland, Wyrens began hybridizing. By 1994, he had produced 1,187 seedlings from his crosses. Among the very few that he named are: 'March Sun' (*R. caucasicum* x 'Moonstone'), a low growing, compact plant with yellow flowers and red blotch; 'Jan-Di-Lyn' ([*R. lacteum* x 'Mary Swaythling'] x 'Ole Olson') with flowers of light yellow shading to pink in the throat; 'Peach Loderi' (Osbo's apricot no. 3 x 'Loderi King George') with trusses of eleven trumpet-shaped flowers in apricot and pink and spotted maroon in throat; and 'Celestial Bells' (Fabia Group x [*R. wardii* x *R. souliei*]), a low, bushy plant with apricot fading to light yellow flowers.

"My rhododendron hobby has added immense joy to my life," Wyrens said (Wyrens, personal communication).

While many Washington hybridizers were aiming for voluptuous blooms on their rhododendrons, when James Caperci came to Seattle from Boston in 1920 he sought out parents that would create small alpines for the rock garden. At his Rainier Mountain Alpine Rhododendron Gardens in south Seattle, which he started in

Berg

James Caperci

1946 and which also sold dwarf conifers, Caperci looked to the lepidotes for parents. He obtained hundreds of packets of rare rhododendron seed and scions from Britain and Japan. When customers purchased plants from him, they always received a free plant—a rare species if you showed an interest. He also made generous donations to the Rhododendron Species Foundation and the Washington Park Arboretum.

Caperci's 'Maricee' (*R. sargentianum* x unknown), once thought to be a selection of *Rhododendron sargentianum*, is a dwarf plant with shiny leaves and white flowers. 'Ernie Dee' (*R. dauricum* x *R. racemosum*), named after his friend Ernest Dzurick, grows to about 2 feet (0.5 m) to a cush-

Greer

'Maricee'

Anderson

Edwin "Ted" Anderson

ion shape and bears violet, frilled flowers. His 18-inch (45 cm) high 'Carousel' (*R. minus* var. *minus* x *R. saluenense*) has small, ball-shaped trusses of pink.

James Caperci received the American Rhododendron Society Gold Medal in 1974.

Leonard Frisbie of Tacoma, founder of the Pacific Rhododendron Society in 1949 (see Chapter 4) and knowledgeable in botany, is most remembered for the "lessons" in botany he gave to the early members of the society he founded and for his observations of *Rhododendron occidentale* in the wild (see Chapter 8). He was primarily interested in the species; however, he also selected and named the Puyallup Valley Group of Mollis azalea seedlings, grown by Gregg McKinnon of Sumner, Washington.

In the mid 1960s, Edwin "Ted" Anderson of Longview, Washington, a retired high school principal, was inspired by Leonard Frisbie to try his hand at hybridizing. His most well-known cross is 'Betty Anderson' ('Van Nes Sensation' x 'Wilburn'), with red-violet flowers, darker and

striped on the reverse. The same cross produced 'Bonnie Snaza' with lilac flowers and red spots. His cross 'Esther Wagner' ([*R. yakushimanum* x 'Earl of Athlone'] x [*R. yakushimanum* x 'Earl of Athlone']) has funnel-shaped, frilly pink flowers and red spots in the throat.

Van Veen

'Betty Anderson'

THE SECOND GENERATION
OF HYBRIDIZERS

In Tacoma—home of Lester Brandt, Hjalmar Larson, and Leonard Frisbie—Joe Davis, like so many other Washington hybridizers who started in the 1960s and 1970s, was encouraged by the earlier hybridizers. Davis, a flower bulb specialist for J. M. McConkey & Co., first purchased rhododendron seed from Hjalmar Larson and grew on some of his crosses. Inspired with the results, Davis used some of them to create his own impressive hybrids. Larson's 'Orange Marmalade' was crossed with Lem's 'Lem's Cameo' to produce Davis's 'Mavis Davis' named after his wife. This upright but spreading plant has stunning light yellow flowers with orange-red edges. 'Cranberry Swirl' ('Lem's Cameo' x 'Coronation Day'), a low growing, spreading plant, bears flowers of a complex colors, starting violet-red in bud and opening to dark purple-pink with a red blotch in the throat. Using another of Larson's hybrids as seed parent, he produced 'Unique Marmalade' ('Orange Marmalade' x 'Unique'), a low growing plant with glossy leaves and red buds opening to wavy-edged pink flowers with and orange throat. In building on the receding generation of hybrids, Davis created hybrids in a startling combination of flower colors—and carrying complicated pedigrees. His hybrids indicate that the West Coast hybridizers were indeed trying for superior rather than repetitious crosses. Joe Davis died in 1996 after contributing not only lovely new rhododendrons but also his time and energy to the American Rhododendron Society, the Pacific Rhododendron Society, and the Rhododendron Species Foundation.

Richard Mauritsen of Tacoma developed the Mauritsen Hybrid Group of evergreen azaleas using the cross ('Hahn's Red' x 'Ward's Ruby').

All are heavy bloomers with single flowers. Among them are: 'Cherry Delight', red; 'Dragon Lady', red-orange; 'Last Tango', bright-red; 'Morning Fire', dark red; 'Orange Daiquiri', red-orange. His elepidote cross 'Buttermint' ('Unique' x [Fabia Group x *R. dichroanthum* ssp. *apodectum*]) has dense foliage on a compact plant flowering in yellow.

Cecil Seabrook of Tacoma produced a number of named hybrids. Of those still on the market the most well-known is 'Grace Seabrook' ('The Honourable Jean Marie de Montague' x *R. strigillosum*), blooming early with bright red flowers and attractive indumented foliage—similar to Frank Mossman's superb 'Taurus' except for the red growth buds. Seabrook also used *R. strigillosum* as a parent for 'Paul Lincke' (Glamour Group x *R. strigillosum*) that also has bright red flowers. Another good red, 'Johnny Bender' ('The Honourable Jean Marie de Montague' x Indiana Group), has heavily textured, glossy foliage. The low growing 'Robert Louis Stevenson' (May Day Group x 'Jester') bears small bright red flowers set off with glossy foliage.

Fred Minch of Tacoma first became interested in rhododendrons in the most unlikely of places—from customers while tending bar in

Minch

Jean and Fred Minch

the 1960s. At first his hybridizing goals were large flowers in unusual colors, but they changed to the more difficult goals of heat and cold tolerance and mildew resistance. In his quest for cold hardiness, he has used *Rhododendron brachycarpum*, and for heat and humidity tolerance in evergreen azaleas he has used 'Pres. F. D. Roosevelt'. Another goal has been plants of compact form in a variety of flower colors. Among his named elepidote crosses are: 'Jeanie's Black Heart' of unknown parentage, with black-red buds opening to dark red flowers on a low growing plant hardy to 0°F (-18°C); 'Oh! Kitty' is also of unknown parentage, with red buds opening to large pink, wavy, fragrant flowers with a red throat, also hardy to 0°F (-18°C). Among his named decidous azalea crosses are: 'Jean's Old Spice' and 'Puyallup Centennial', with double orange flowers.

Fred and his wife, Jean, have been active in the American Rhododendron Society and the Azalea Society of America.

Olympia, Washington, also became a center for hybridizing. Fred Peste of Olympia took advantage of the fine form and foliage of *Rhododendron degronianum* ssp. *yakushimanum* in his hybrid creations. 'Barry Rodgers' (*R. degronianum* ssp. *yakushimanum* x 'Doncaster') has pink, frilled flowers with dark edges in a large truss on a low growing plant. 'Fred Peste' ([*R. degronianum* ssp. *yakushimanum* x 'Corona'] x *R. haematodes*) bears red flowers with a maroon throat and indumented leaves on a low growing plant. The same cross produced 'Marlene Peste', with red flowers and glossy leaves on a well-rounded plant. 'Lillian Peste' (*R. degronianum* ssp. *yakushimanum* 'Koichiro Wada' x unknown) bears pink, yellow, and orange flowers on a low plant. This hybrid selfed produced 'Martha Peste' with yellow-pink flowers and indumented foliage. His most

well-known hybrid, however, is 'Centennial Celebration' ('Purple Lace' x *R. degronianum* ssp. *yakushimanum*) bearing frilly, light orchid flowers with a spot of green on the upper petal and with leathery foliage. It was named in honor of Washington State's centennial.

John Holden of Olympia used the fragrant 'Polar Bear' to produce a number of hybrids, two of which are still in the market. The highly fragrant 'Carol Amelia' ('Polar Bear' x 'Evening Glow') has white flowers with yellow overtones and red spotting. 'Mrs. A. J. Holden' of the same cross also bears fragrant flowers but yellow with a pink edge and light green spots.

Alma Manenica of Olympia named only two of her crosses, one of which is on the market, 'Heart's Delight' ('Mrs. A. T. de la Mare' x 'Britannia'), with bright red flowers and dark red in the throat and dense foliage on a well-shaped plant.

Roy Clark of Olympia produced a number of hybrids, including 'Olympic Knight' (Fabia Group x unknown) flowering in dark red with a darker red blotch.

Walter Elliott, the owner of a furniture store in Shelton, Washington after serving in the military during World War II, was stricken by the "rhodie virus" in 1956 when he and his wife, Vera, were given a rhododendron as a gift. He began collecting the old English hybrids when William Whitney suggested that he start a chapter of the American Rhododendron Society in Shelton, which he did with the help of Hjalmar Larson and Carl Fawcett of Tacoma. (Carl Fawcett introduced several crosses by Lem, Ostbo, and Brandt and was doing his own hybridizing with yellow, although he did not register any names of his own crosses.) The give-and-take of this rhododendron group added to Elliott's enthusiasm for hybridizing his own plants.

Goheen

'Cinquero'

Walter Elliott considered his best accomplishments 'Vera Elliott' ('Lemon Custard' x 'Crest'), using his own hybrid as seed parent to produce a large plant with dark pink flowers spotted with red; 'George Sweesy' ('Vera Elliott' x 'Dr. A. Blok') with pink, wavy-edged flowers spotted with brown; and 'Odd Ball' (China Group x 'Goldbug') with red flowers and terracotta spotting on a broad plant.

David Goheen of Camas, Washington, a research chemist by profession, became interested in rhododendrons in 1960 through Ben Lancaster, also of Camas. Lancaster became his rhododendron mentor and introduced him to the limitless possibilities of hybridizing. Surpris-

Goheen

'Estacada'

ingly, it was also through Lancaster that Dave Goheen discovered that the late David Leach was his cousin.

Goheen used the 'Koichiro Wada' form of the species *Rhododendron degronianum* ssp. *yakushimanum* for a number of his crosses still on the market, producing nicely rounded, low growing plants in a variety of flower colors.

Goheen

'Neat-O'

Goheen

'Durango'

'Cinquero' ('Koichiro Wada' x R. *strigillosum*) has indumented foliage bearing orange-red flowers and red spotting in the throat. 'Estacada' ('Koichiro Wada' x R. *arboreum*) has red buds opening to dark pink flowers and convex leaves with white indumentum. 'Frango'

Goheen

'Cuarto'

('Koichiro Wada' x 'Noyo Chief') bears fragrant pink flowers with orange spotting. His well-known 'Neat-O' (R. *campanulatum* x 'Koichiro Wada') has light pink flowers and dark green, indumented foliage.

Goheen's 'Senora Meldon' ('Lackamas Blue' x 'Blue Diamond') is an upright, dense plant bearing small violet-blue flowers and aromatic foliage. His 'Jalipeno' ([Fabia Group x R. *haematodes*] x ['Earl of Athlone' x 'The Honourable Jean Marie de Montague']), a low grower to about 30 inches (75 cm) in ten years, bears bright red flowers spotted brown. Three crosses recently registered and introduced by

A Sandy Rhododendron of Sandy, Oregon, are: 'Durango' ('Ruby Bowman' x R. *elliotii* 'War Paint'), with wavy-edged flowers purple pink of the inside and purple-red on the outside and of dense habit; 'Tabasco's Sister' ('Frango' x 'Estacada') with flowers of red-orange inside and red outside and of dense habit; and 'Tracigo's Sister' (R. *degronianum* ssp. *yakushimanum* x R. *sperabile*) with flowers pale yellowish pink inside and deep yellow-pink outside and of dense habit.

Goheen served as president of the Rhododendron Species Foundation and received the Gold Medal from the American Rhododendron Society in 1988.

Vernon "Bud" Wyatt of Union, Washington, a Christmas tree grower, grocery store owner, and nurseryman during various stages in his life, eventually became involved in hybridizing. Among his named crosses are 'Mary Briggs' (R. *haematodes* x 'Elizabeth'), a low growing plant with dark red flowers, the azaleodendron 'Hazel Smith' (R. *occidentale* x 'Corona'), with white flowers and a red blotch, and 'Elfin Hill' ('Jock' x R. *haematodes*), a compact plant with pink flowers.

Dr. Frank Mossman, an ophthalmologist from Vancouver, Washington, was the best friend the genus *Rhododendron* could have, seeking out the pioneers who knew it best and introducing numerous neophytes to its seductive embrace. In describing his first encounter with the genus, he writes: "In the 1950s, I became interested in rhododendrons and, like most people, I planted a red, a pink, a purple, and a magenta—namely 'The Honourable Jean Marie de Montague', 'Pink Pearl', 'Purple Splendour', and 'Cynthia'" (Mossman, personal communication). The bad freeze of 1955 dampened his rhododendron interests until one day in the late 1950s he took a cataract from Ben

Goheen

Dr. David Goheen with Prof. Fang, Wen-Pei of the University of Sichuan

Goheen

'Taurus'

Goheen

'Washington Centennial'

Lancaster's eye. Lancaster invited him to his nursery and gave him a plant of 'Snow Lady', which eventually grew to 2 feet (0.5 m) tall and 6 feet (2 m) wide. Through the kindly Lancaster, Mossman was soon drawn into the rhododendron milieu.

Lancaster taught the young doctor how to hybridize, how to collect and store pollen, and how to put pollen on the stigma. Mossman, in turn, took Lancaster's pollen of 'Evening Glow', a new, yellow flowering plant, which Lancaster used to create his 'Ben Lancaster'. Mossman recalls numerous people who, like himself, were influenced by Lancaster: David Goheen of Camas, Washing-

Goheen

R. strigillosum

ton, Tom McGuire of Portland, Dr. Forrest Bump of Forest Grove, Oregon, and Edwin T. Anderson of Longview, Washington.

In Mossman's years of hybridizing, he believes he has one "standout" production—'Taurus' ('The Honourable Jean Marie de Montague' x *R. strigillosum*). Judging from its long-time popularity, the gardening public agrees with his assessment.

After Mossman was introduced to *Rhododendron occidentale* by Leonard Frisbie (see Chapter 8), he used it as a parent, discovering that it will cross with elepidote rhododendrons and many of the azalea species if it is used as the seed parent. He also found that intraspecific crosses of selected clones of *R. occidentale* sometimes have the orange or yellow-orange color on the upper two or three petals and occasionally on all petals. When these types are crossed with one another, this feature comes out in the progeny. For example, one clone (SM #30) with yellow on all petals produced progeny with orange on all petals. The tendency tends to come out when it is crossed with other azaleas, both species and Knap Hill azaleas. The *R. occidentale* clone 'Stagecoach

Frills' when crossed with David Leach's find of *R. calendulaceum* 'Colossus' produces in the first generation some fine flower forms with the golden Marigold-type coppery yellow color typical of *R. calendulaceum* but with the frilled flowers of 'Stagecoach Frills'. His 'Washington Centennial' ([*R. occidentale* x *R. bakeri*] x 'Santiam') opens from orange-yellow buds to light orange-yellow flowers. When *R. occidentale* is crossed with elepidotes, the leaf tends to be more leathery than the azalea species, with flower shape and color not normally seen in the azalea. It is Mossman's theory that when an intraspecific cross of *R. occidentale* produces an azaleodeondron-like plant, there is some *R. macrophyllum* in the background. The two species bloom side by side in the coastal areas. One attribute of *R. occidentale* is its resistance to root rot, and in addition Mossman is working for mildew resistance in his hybridizing with *R. occidentale* crossed with the Knap Hill azaleas and using unusual forms of *R. occidentale* with the Knap Hills for interesting plants.

Mossman has also used the elepidote West Coast native *R. macrophyllum* 'Seven Devils' crossed with 'Purple Splendour' to produce progeny with bell-shaped, waxy, wine-red flowers.

Cavender

Britt Smith and Dr. Frank Mossman

The rhododendron interests of Britt Smith of Kent, Washington, span many areas including hunting for superior forms of *Rhododendron occidentale* in the wild with Frank Mossman, plant exploring in Sikkim (see Chapter 8)—and hybridizing. After his retirement in the late 1950s from a career in aeronautical engineering, Smith was looking for a hobby to give him pleasure during the next stage of his life. Dr. Frank Mossman provided the answer. When Britt and his wife, Jean, moved to a new house in Kent, Mossman brought them rhododendrons for landscaping. He also introduced him to Hjalmar Larson, Lester Brandt, Halfdan Lem, William Whitney, Ben Nelson, Roy and Honoré Hacanson, most of retirement age and "having a whee of a time hybridizing" (Smith, personal communication). As a result, Smith began his own hybridizing program, aiming for yellow flowers and better plants. Among approximately ten named crosses, he considers some of his most successful: 'Hawaiian Holiday' ('Senorita' x 'Autumn Gold'), with flowers of light purple-pink shading to a yellow center and a red blotch; 'Britton Hill Bugle' ('Karkov' x 'Red Loderi') with large trusses of bugle-shaped

Cavender

Rhododendron occidentale

dark red flowers and a dark blotch; and 'Jean Eleanor' (*R. lacteum* x 'Jingle Bells'), a wide low-growing plant with light yellow-green flowers.

In the mid 1960s, Frank Mossman took Smith down another rhododendron path—pursuing the native West Coast azalea *Rhododendron occidentale*. Intrigued by Leonard Frisbie's discourse on this wild azalea in a publication by the Pacific Rhododendron Society (Frisbie 1961), Smith and Mossman set out May 27, 1966, on their first trip to "occidentale land" in Oregon and California. They investigated this beautiful native for some sixteen years (see Chapter 8).

As a result of witnessing the variation among *Rhododendron occidentale* species in the wild, Smith became interested in the possibility of variation in the Himalayan species, which led to an unusual and gratifying friendship with rhododendron enthusiasts in Sikkim and subsequent trips to the country (see Chapter 8).

Smith has been active in the American Rhododendron Society and the Rhododendron Species Foundation, receiving a Gold Medal from the former for his wide-ranging interests and contributions.

In the Seattle area, Garda Griswold of Kirkland, a mortgage banker, grew up at the family owned Griswold Nursery of Seattle, where she was in charge of azalea cuttings at age 14 and developed an affinity for them. By the early 1970s, inspired by her mother who hybridized rhododendrons, she tried her luck at hybridizing evergreen azaleas. Out of her first group of crosses came 'Dhabi' ('Vuyk's Rosyred' x 'Moonbeam', a Glenn Dale), with flowers of dark purple-pink and red spotting. Much against her father's wishes, this cross was named after her ailing cat, which recovered after the name was registered. The same parents produced 'Pamela Malland' with flowers of purple-pink, light pink in throat,

Griswold

Garda Griswold

and red spotting, and 'Orine Holm' and 'Rosy Cheeks'. Using a Satsuki as seed parent and the same Glenn Dale as pollen parent, she produced 'Laura Holm' ('Wako' x 'Moonbeam').

Griswold approaches hybridizing as a "relaxing hobby. . . just to be able to create a nice plant—flower and foliage—is a reward" (Griswold, personal communication).

Bob Korn of Seattle registered the name of only two of his crosses, one of them the admired 'Phyllis Korn' ('Diane' x 'Gomer Waterer'), an upright and well-branched plant with white flowers and red blotch.

Edwin Weber of Seattle was hybridizing in the 1970s, producing mostly purple flowering plants still on the market. His 'Abe Arnott' ('Marchioness of Lansdowne' x 'Lee's Dark Purple') is a two-toned purple with a dark flare. 'Edwin O. Weber' ('Purpureum Elegans' x 'Madame Albert Moser') bears purple flowers with a green blotch in a large truss. 'Ruth A. Weber' ('Marchioness of Lansdowne' x 'Old Port') bears flowers of bright purple with dark spots in large trusses.

Mrs. Howard Beck of Seattle produced three hybrids still in the market with the cross ('Loderi Venus' x 'Anna'). 'Markeeta's Flame' has deep green leaves, red leaf stems, and rose-red flowers. Her 'Markeeta's Prize' with thick waxy leaves bears bright red flowers. 'Queen Nefertiti' bears dark pink flowers with dark edges.

LaVern Freimann of Bellingham, Washington, a professional horticulturist and lily breeder, also became involved in hybridizing rhododendrons. Three of his crosses resulted from (*R. degronianum* ssp. *yakushimanum* x Leo Group), but his most well known is 'Molly Ann' ('Elizabeth' x unknown), a dense, compact plant that grows to about 3 feet (1 m) with round leaves and pink flowers. The plant was introduced in 1973 and is still on the market.

Sigrid Laxdall, also of Bellingham, named six of her crosses, one of which is still on the market: 'Dan Laxdall' ('Elizabeth' x 'Mrs. G. W. Leak'), with pink flowers and dark pink in the throat and up the center of the flower lobes.

Another Bellingham hybridizer, J. Freeman Stephens, produced 'Freeman R. Stephens' and 'Douglas R. Stephens' from a cross of 'The Honourable Jean Marie de Montague' with an unnamed white hybrid, both with large red flowers and high, conical trusses and glossy leaves.

Harold and Morna Stockman of Port Angeles, Washington, were busily hybridizing in the 1970s and 1980s. Their long list of named crosses is testament to their intense hybridizing activity. They made frequent use of 'Purple Splendour' as a parent for their creations, one of which is 'Christie S.' ('Evening Glow' x 'Purple Splendour') with orchid-rose flowers and gold center and maroon flare.

In 1979, a group of nine members of the Seattle Chapter founded the Northwest Rhododendron Hybridizers' Group. The first meeting was held at the home of Elsie Watson, with Robert Badger chairing. Among its activities was rating rhododendron trusses. At the test garden at the Meerkerk Rhododendron Gardens this knowledgeable group, skills honed by their own hybridizing, rated the plants on truss, foliage and plant habit.

Traditionally the group decides upon a "cross of the year." One or two members make the cross and distribute seed to the group to grow on. One of the results of this group effort was 'Coral Pacific' ('Lem's Tangerine' x 'Pacific Gold'), a plant grown by member Paul Christensen and featured at the American Rhododendron Society's annual convention in Bellevue, Washington in 1999.

Stewart

'Phyllis Korn'

The Northwest Hybridizers' Group continues to meet. Among the active members are Elsie
Watson, Frank Fujioka, and Pat Halligan, all
mentioned above. "We all feel a close bond of
mutual interest in our wonderful world of rhododendrons," Watson wrote about the group
(Watson, personal communication).

By the end of the 1980s, hybridizing in
Washington had gained great momentum,
founded on the achievements of the early hybridizers and accelerated by the innovations
of their followers.

CHAPTER 7

THE HYBRIDIZERS OF
BRITISH COLUMBIA & CALIFORNIA

North and south of the Oregon-Washington centers of rhododendron activity, hybridizers were mixing genes to create plants suitable for their own climates. The first named rhododendron cross was, in fact, made on Vancouver Island in British Columbia by George Fraser, and the island's growers continued to be seduced by the possibilities the mild climate afforded. On the British Columbia mainland, growers soon were drawn into the hybridizing venture, creating ever more various and complex crosses. In California, the climates offered both obstacles and opportunities for rhododendron hybridizing. In southern California, growers turned to the heat tolerant evergreen azaleas and vireyas, and in northern California the *Maddenia* species, which tolerated only minor freezes, and the relatively tender large-leaf species were used to create large-flowered, fragrant hybrids. The va-

ARS Journal

'George Fraser'

riety within the genus enabled the whole West Coast to take part in the rhododendron hybridizing adventure.

THE HYBRIDIZERS OF BRITISH COLUMBIA

Before the great interest in rhododendrons had gathered momentum in British Columbia, one man in relative isolation on Vancouver Island began taking his chances in the rhododendron hybridizing gamble. The pioneer rhododendron grower George Fraser made the first documented cross on the West Coast when the *Rhododendron canadense* he received in a shipment of cranberry plants from Nova Scotia bloomed in about 1912. He crossed it with *R. molle* ssp. *japonicum*. The result, the Fraseri Group, bears rose-lilac flowers and is still in cultivation. In his hybridizing efforts, Fraser relied greatly on primary crosses, especially the native North American species. In approximately 1922, Fraser crossed the West Coast native azalea *R. occidentale* with the East Coast native *R. arborescens*, which resulted in the John Blair Group, bearing pure white flowers with dark pink anthers and stamens and named after his friend, the landscape architect John Blair. Also in the 1920s, using the West Coast native elepidote *R. macrophyllum* and the Asian *R. arboreum*, he produced 'Mrs. Jamie Fraser' ([*R. arboreum* x *R. macrophyllum*] x *R. arboreum*), with dark red flowers and a flare of black spots in the throat. Around 1930 Fraser made two crosses, one with two native North American elepidotes resulting in 'Maxie' (*R. maximum* x *R. macrophyllum*) with pink flowers, and one with the East Coast native elepidote *R. catawbiense* and an English hybrid, resulting in 'Camich' (*R. catawbiense* x 'Michael Waterer'), with dark red-purple flowers. His last registered cross and probably the most well known was 'Albert Close' (*R. maximum* x *R. macrophyllum*), with bright pink flowers. In his isolation on the west coast of Vancouver Island, Fraser relied on communication by letter with Joseph Gable to exchange information on their mutual passion—

hybridizing rhododendrons. Bill Dale of Sidney, British Columbia, on Vancouver Island, has developed a collection of the Fraser hybrids.

Fraser's specific hybridizing goals were to produce attractive, salable hybrids which would be hardy away from the mild British Columbia coastal climate. He also used the West Coast native *R. occidentale* as a parent plant in order to get fragrant offspring. Fraser wanted to be able to sell his hybrids before they were of blooming size and yet be absolutely confident of their color. In the course of his hybridizing, Fraser discovered that hybrids that were sterile often became fertile with age—information that Gable took to heart.

Even though their great love was species, the pioneer rhododendron growers Ted and Mary Greig of Royston, British Columbia, on Vancouver Island also became involved in hybridizing, using Asian species and English hybrids. Their primary crosses include: the yellow flowered 'Butterball' (*R. xanthostephanum* x *R. triflorum*); the rose flowered 'Mary Greig' (*R. neriiflorum* ssp. *neriiflorum* x *R. souliei*); the rose flowered 'Royston Festival' (*R. auriculatum* x *R. kyawi*); and 'Ted Greig' (*R. campylocarpum* x *R. fortunei* ssp. *discolor*). Their 'Royston Red' (*R. forrestii* ssp. *forrestii* Repens Group x *R. thomsonii*) bears dark red flowers on a compact plant with attractive round leaves.

Goheen

'Royston Red'

They also brought English hybrids into their program to produce: the rose flowered 'Last Rose' (*R. fortunei* ssp. *discolor* x 'Tally Ho'); the bright yellow flowered 'Royal Anne' ('Azor' x unnamed hybrid); the yellow, red-edged flowered 'Royston Reverie' (*R. auriculatum* x Fabia Group); and 'Veronica Milner' (*R. campylocarpum* x 'Little Ben'). The late flowering, fragrant species *R. auriculatum*, discovered by Augustine Henry in 1885 in China, played a major role in their hybridizing, and one begins to see a pattern develop. They crossed it with their own 'Last Rose' to produce the white and rose flowered 'Royston Rose' ('Last Rose' x *R. auriculatum*) and 'Royston Summertime' (*R. auriculatum* x 'Last Rose'). The Ted and Mary Greig Garden in Stanley Park, Vancouver, British Columbia, features their *R. auriculatum* crosses.

The exquisite 'Canada' (of unknown parentage but likely including *Rhododendron campylogynum*), with small tubular flowers and round leaves on a compact plant perfect for the rock garden, has been erroneously attributed to the Greigs. 'Canada' came to the Greigs from the Sunningdale Nursery in England and grown at the Royston Nursery. In a letter to Stuart Holland Mary Greig wrote: "Caperci's (plant) came from Sunningdale via us. I expect it was an accidental cross. I never made any campylogynum cross" (Holland 1989). The alpine expert James Caperci of Seattle named it.

The Greigs made a large number of crosses, but many of these were lost when they were sold in 1965 to the Vancouver Parks Board during a strike of government employees. The little plants succumbed to lack of water while stored in a greenhouse.

Albert de Mezey of Victoria developed a fine garden at Kildonan where he restored a mansion after its wartime use as military quarters. He obtained rhododendrons from the Layritz Nursery, the Greigs, and English nurseries for his garden and his hybridizing. "My own best hybrids used the Greig form of *R. campylocarpum*, yellow with a red eye," he said (Leslie and Frank Drew 1989). Yet one of his best hybrids, at least according to Norman Todd of Victoria, is his 'Mary's Favourite' (*R. williamsianum* x *R. wardii*), a cross he made in 1953. It is consistently floriferous with bell-shaped flowers born at every growing point with five to six flowers in a truss. The attractive leaves are the round williamsianum-type leaf. The plant can grow to 6 feet (2 m) tall.

Stuart Holland of Vancouver Island, at one time the Chief Geologist for British Columbia, was fascinated with botany and, in particular, rhododendrons, growing them and hybridizing them at his home on Transit Street in Victoria. One of his best hybrids is 'Transit Gold' ('Royal Flush', cream form x *R. cinnabarinum* ssp. *xanthocodon*) with yellow funnel-shaped flowers of heavy substance in lax trusses. Other unnamed seedlings of this cross grew in Holland's garden and exhibited a variety of flower color.

Evelyn Weesjes of Sidney on Vancouver Island grew on a number of Hjalmar Larson's crosses during the 1960s when she was a propagator for the University of British Columbia

Weesjes

Evelyn Weesjes and Mary Greig

rhododendron collection. Along with cuttings of English hybrids, Larson had added some of his own crosses, presumably for testing outside his nursery location in Tacoma, Washington. Weesjes weeded out the obviously inferior clones, and Larson would come up to evaluate them. Several of the batch were eventually named.

Weesjes says she herself is not a hybridizer, although she has made crosses "that didn't result in anything that was of any merit except for two that I may register some day" (Weesjes, personal communication). She related an anecdote that describes a method of hybridizing that might happen more often than hybridizers admit. "As sometimes happens, the planned crosses may come up duds while the happenstance ones a winner. Such was the case when I dashed out with Larson's 'Mrs. Horace Fogg' truss to find a mate for it and dabbed pollen on the first thing in sight which happened to be 'Van Nes Sensation' . . . Nick [my husband] all the time waiting impatiently for me as we took off on holiday" (Weesjes, personal communication). She has registered and introduced a number of Hjalmar Larson's crosses. In 1970 she made the cross resulting in the hybrid 'Doctor Bonar Buffam' (*R. arboreum* ssp. *delavayi* x *R. barbatum*).

Justice

Dr. Robert C. Rhodes

Dr. Robert Rhodes of Gabriola Island, British Columbia, was introduced to rhododendrons by Gerald Charlton, a native of Maple Ridge and a landscape architect, who designed a garden with rhododendrons and flowering cherries at the hospital with which Rhodes was associated. He also helped Rhodes plan a garden at his Maple Ridge home and in 1959 introduced him to the American Rhododendron Society. Rhodes then met high school principal Eric Langton, some of whose rhododendron crosses Rhodes grew on. One of these was 'Norma Hodge' (unknown x Fabia Group) with pink flowers and a red blotch radiating in a spotted flare.

By the 1960s and 1970s, Rhodes started making his own crosses. "I found growing plants on the large property we owned in Maple Ridge, where I practiced medicine, a wonderful retreat from the stress of my work" (Rhodes, personal communication). At the same time he grew seed from the American Rhododendron Society seed exchange, both hand-pollinated crosses from

Weesjes

'Nick's Choice'

Haida Gold Gardens

'Haida Gold'

around the world and species from the wild as well as seed and seedlings from other hybridizers—Robert Bovee, William Whitney, John Lofthouse, Milton Wildfong and others. He made several selections from these sources, one of which was the lovely 'Haida Gold' (*R. wardii* x Goldfort Group), with dark green leaves and bright yellow flowers on a low growing plant, a cross by Bovee. Another was 'Sierra Treasure' ('Crest' x *R. lacteum*), a cross by John Lofthouse with fragrant, wavy yellow flowers and a maroon blotch and dark green concave leaves. He also has selected forms of *R. davidsonianum* and *R. russatum*.

Of Rhodes's crosses on the market, the most well-known is the lepidote cross 'Bob's Blue' ('Ilam Violet' x 'Blue Diamond'). It bears bright blue flowers on a compact plant, and its deep green leaves turn maroon in winter. His 'Jean Rhodes' ('Naomi' x 'Mrs. Horace Fogg') bears bright pink flowers, darker in the throat, in trusses of fourteen.

Since these crosses were made, Rhodes moved to Gabriola Island and built a new garden where he continues to select seedlings brought from his garden in Maple Ridge.

One of the earliest rhododendron growers on the mainland of British Columbia was Dr. C. S. McKee. While invalided during his medical services in WWI, he visited the Royal Botanic Garden, Edinburgh, and met plant explorer George Forrest. After returning to Vancouver he received seed from Edinburgh, growing on thousands of plants. Although he left breeding to Mother Nature, he produced a group of plants hardy for the area with good foliage and general appearance. The Fraser South Chapter of the American Rhododendron Society has attempted to catalogue and take cuttings of some of the McKee plants.

On the mainland, Milton Wildfong of Mission, British Columbia, opened Silver Creek Gardens in the mid 1960s, specializing in rhododendrons. As a member of the Vancouver Rhododendron Society (Vancouver Chapter of the American Rhododendron Society), he

Rhodes

'Bob's Blue'

Cook

Milton Wildfong and Alleyne Cook

advised members on pollen and seed collection, contributed generously to the ARS seed exchange, and was the new Fraser Valley Chapter's chief mentor.

In 1968, Wildfong began hybridizing, although he admitted to few early successes because of insufficient knowledge of genetic pedigrees of parent plants. Among his goals were better yellow-flowering rhododendrons and hardiness for his region. He often said, "If it's not hardy it's not worth growing" (Gerald Heriot, personal communication). In later years his goals expanded to attractive foliage with indumentum, using species coupled with hybrids to produce hardy, yellow-flowering, indumented plants. 'Ruffles and Frills' ('Hydon Glow' x 'Lem's Cameo') was a realization of most of these goals. The frilled, fragrant yellow flowers have pink edges and red in the throat. The reverse side of the petals is pink. This large plant carries domed trusses of twelve flowers. Its leaves are heavily textured and bronze in new growth. 'Snugbug' ('Sangreal' x *R. tsariense*) bears red, funnel-shaped flowers fading to pink held in a wide truss.

John Lofthouse of Vancouver, a businessman by profession, lifted rhododendron hybridizing to a new level in British Columbia—and in the Northwest. His first goals of perfect, fuller trusses, better foliage, and longer blooming periods together with later goals of longer flowers shaped like trumpets with reflexed calyxes have been mostly realized after some forty years of hybridizing.

Preparation for his hybridizing achievements, however, began long before he began dabbing rhododendron pollen. His father grew ornamentals and vegetables and competed in horticultural shows in Vancouver, and two uncles were botanists who collected herbarium specimens and plants for the British Museum and the Royal Horticultural Society. After mar-

Justice

John G. Lofthouse

riage and acquiring a home, his first priority was developing a garden. Then he obtained a greenhouse where he could develop his interest in propagation and hybridizing. He worked with roses, chrysanthemums, carnations, and African violets. He spent five years on eliminating powdery mildew from tuberous begonias and, also during this time, began hybridizing rhododendrons. In 1964 his rhododendron hybrid 'Pink Petticoats' ('Jan Dekens' x 'Britannia') came into bloom—a plant that fulfilled his first goal of perfect, fuller trusses. This plant bears frilly pink flowers in very large trusses. Its attractive leaves curl downward and are longer than wide. The well-known and distinctive 'One Thousand Butterflies' ('Lem's Cameo' x 'Pink Petticoats') crosses Halfdan Lem's prize with his own creation to produce large trusses of pink flowers fading to cream in the center with a red butterfly-shaped blotch of red. 'Butter Brickle' ('Hotei' x 'Lem's Cameo') bears flowers of gold with a maroon star radiating to the upper petal and with the calyx and the backside of the flowers in pink. The plant form is compact and new foliage bronze. 'Yellow Petticoats' ('Hotei' x ['Pink Petticoats' x R. wardii, selfed]) bears frilly yellow flowers on a compact plant with dark green leaves. The large-growing 'Sierra Sunrise' ('Mrs. Horace Fogg' x 'Point Defiance') has pink ruffled flowers in tall, conical trusses and pointed leaves that turn upwards from the midrib.

With the goal of producing better foliage, Lofthouse used a primary cross to create 'Magic Moments' (R. aberconwayi x R. degronianum ssp. yakushimanum) with shiny green foliage on a compact plant blooming in white flowers with a maroon blotch. 'Enticement' ('Sunup Sundown' x 'Lem's Cameo') has a low growing form tolerant of shade and sun, with red buds opening to pink flowers with pink rays and orange-red spotting in the throat. 'Supergold' ('Hotei' x 'Joanita') has an attractive form with nice green foliage and yellow flowers. 'Sierra del Oro' ('Crest' x R. lacteum) bears trusses of light yellow flowers with wavy, reflexed lobes lasting four to six weeks. The plant is wider than tall with arching branches. The goal of longer flowers was achieved with Lofthouse's newer hybrids: 'Silver Trumpets' ('Sunup Sundown' x Whitney hybrid) with lily-shaped flowers of plum color fading to white with blotched throat; and 'Jeda' ('Butter Brickle' x ['Sunup Sundown' x Whitney hybrid]) with orange flowers. Lofthouse has produced many other named crosses and continues to hybridize.

Besides his many hybrids, John Lofthouse developed a propagating unit known as the "Lofthouse propagator" for use in growing cuttings, using heat lamps and mist (Lofthouse 1987).

John Lofthouse has lectured widely and been actively involved in the Vancouver Rhododendron Society and a member of the International Plant Propagators Society. He received the Silver Medal from the American Rhododendron Society in 1999.

Gordon and Vern Finley of Surrey, British Columbia, are avid hybridizers, winning a competition hosted by the city of Burnaby for a new rhododendron to represent its 1992 centennial celebration. Their prize-winning plant, 'Burnaby Centennial' ('Leona' x 'Etta Burrows'), bears compact trusses of fourteen to sixteen five-lobed flowers of raspberry red with lighter red stamens and style and black anthers. Its foliage is pointed, medium in size, and shiny dark green.

Other British Columbian hybridizers and growers of note are Ed J. Trayling, Dr. Bobby Ogdon, Dr. Margaret (Mike) Trembeth, Ken Gibson, Dr. J. S. Marcellus, and Norbeth Wuenche.

Les Clay, a nurseryman in Langley, British Columbia, and a strong supporter of the American Rhododendron Society, is responsible for making many of the new British Columbia hybrids available to the public.

THE HYBRIDIZERS OF CALIFORNIA

The Nuccio Nursery of Altadena in southern California developed the Nuccio Hybrid Group, a group of hardy evergreen azaleas for the garden and for forcing. The family nursery, founded by Julius and Joe Nuccio in 1935, is continued by the founder's nephew Julius, Jr., and his two sons, Tom and

The Nuccios
Jim, Julius, Tom, Joe and Julius Nuccio Jr.

Jim. Parentage of the Nuccio Group includes the following hybrid groups: Kurume, Satsuki, Rutherford, Belgian Indian, Kerrigan, and Southern Indian. The nursery has developed over seventy-five hybrids in a stunning variety of flower color and shape, plant form, bloom period, and tolerance to sun.

When the Southern California Chapter of the American Rhododendron Society compiled its list of "good doers" for Fred Galle's book Azaleas, several of the Nuccio Hybrid Group were listed. 'Nuccio's Happy Days' ('Purity', Rutherford x 'Louisa Bobbink', Rutherford) bears light purple hose-in hose double flowers and blooms for ten months on a plant of moderate growth. 'Nuccio's Garden Party' of the same cross, with dark pink semi-double flowers 3 inches (7.5 cm) wide, blooms profusely in spring and spot flowering in fall and winter. Plant size is moderate.

The Nuccio's Carnival series owes its parentage to open pollinated 'Red Poppy' from the Kerrigan Hybrid Group. Galle's "good doer" list from the Southern California Chapter included four of these: 'Nuccio's Carnival Queen' bears vivid pink semi-double flowers 2½ inches (6 cm) wide on a plant of low to medium growth. 'Nuccio's Carnival' has dark pink single to semi-double flowers 3½ to 4 inches (9 to 10 cm) wide on a tall plant. 'Nuccio's Carnival Candy' has bright red flowers 3½ to 4 inches (9 to 10 cm) wide on a tall plant. 'Nuccio's Carnival Firecracker' has bright red-orange flowers 2½ inches (6 cm) wide on a tall plant.

Other Nuccio azaleas mentioned by the Southern California Chapter as "good doers" are 'Nuccio's Pink Bubbles' ('Nuccio's California Dawn' x 'Nuccio's Pink Champagne') bearing light pink, double 3-inch (7.5 cm) flowers on a moderate sized plant with large foliage; and

'Nuccio's Allegro' ('Avenir', Belgium Indian x 'Hexe') bearing red semi-double flowers 2½ inches (6 cm) wide on a plant of moderate growth.

Tom Nuccio, a frequent lecturer on the Nuccio Nursery's azaleas and camellias and known for his great enthusiasm, told a meeting of the Southern California Chapter in 1999 that some of their most popular azaleas are 'Nuccio's Happy Days', 'Nuccio's Garden Party', and the Carnival series—the same azaleas appearing on Galle's "good doer" list.

William Moynier of Los Angeles began hybridizing rhododendrons from the subsection *Vireya* in the 1970s after a long, serendipitous journey through the genus looking for plants that would do well in the warm, dry southern California climate. Before the 1960s, Moynier remembers seeing the rhododendrons 'Pink Pearl' and 'Unknown Warrior' but not much more. However, after reading David Leach's *Rhododendrons of the World*, he knew the rhododendron horizon was broader than it appeared. He sought out the nurseries of John Druecker and Paul J. Bowman in Fort Bragg, bringing back some 200 varieties. One out of ten or twenty grew in Moynier's garden. Then he discovered the vireyas, largely through Peter Sullivan at the Strybing Arboretum in San Francisco. Moynier also received seed, pollen, and plants from Dr. Carl Phetteplace, Cecil Smith, Mrs. Edgar Greer, Peter Schick, and Maurice Sumner. Through the American Rhododendron Society seed exchange and its vireya chairman William Moyles, Moynier was able to get seed from international

Moynier

UCLA Botanic Garden

Moynier

Bill Moynier

sources in New Zealand and Australia, where climates were also conducive to vireya culture, and England, where vireyas were grown in greenhouses. Through Moynier's enthusiasm for vireyas, other members of the Southern California Chapter of the American Rhododendron Society began growing them successfully outdoors all year long in the frost-free climate.

By the 1970s Moynier was making his own vireya crosses. Since then he has grown on some 500 batches of seeds from his own and others' crosses. He has named a number of his own crosses. His 'Eastern Zanzibar' (*R. konori* x *R. zoelleri*) bears scented, light yellow flowers with lobes of dark pink in trusses of four to five flowers. 'Avalon' ('Shasta' x *R. aurigeranum*) bears light yellow, wavy-edged flowers in a domed truss

on a compact plant. The long flowering 'Pleasant Companion' (*R. lochiae* x [*R. konori* x 'Dr. Herman Sleumer']) has funnel-shaped fragrant red flowers on a compact plant. 'Sunny's Brother' (*R. christianae* x *R. macgregoriae*) bears bright yellow flowers with red-orange lobes set off by collars of dark green, round leaves. The newly registered 'Jeanhee' ('Felinda' x *R. javanicum*) carries its scented, tubular, yellow-pink flowers in a domed truss. The dark green leaves are up-curved at the margins with tan scales below on a plant of dense habit.

Moynier has registered and introduced many of the hybrids of Peter Sullivan of San Francisco. Among those he registered that are on the market are: 'Aravir' ('Pink Delight' x *R. jasminiflorum*) with fragrant white flowers and attractive foliage; 'Belisar' ([*R. laetum* x *R. zoelleri*] x [*R. macgregoriae* x *R. zoelleri*]), a red-orange and yellow bicolor on a tall-growing plant; 'Cair Paravel' (['Triumphans' x *R. javanicum*] x *R. leucogigas*), a tall-growing plant with shiny leaves and large, ruffled, bright pink flowers; 'Cristo Rey' ([*R. macgregoriae* x *R. zoelleri*] x [*R. laetum* x *R. zoelleri*]), a bicolor with yellow-gold and red-orange tubular flowers in a domed truss on a well-branching plant; and 'Emmanuel' (*R. zoelleri* x *R. javanicum*) with red flowers shading to yellow on a compact plant.

Peter Sullivan was associated with the Strybing Arboretum, helping to develop its vireya collection and making crosses. Among the Sullivan crosses not mentioned above and still on the market are: 'Anastasia' (*R. wrightianum* x [*R. konori* x *R. laetum*]) with red flowers in hanging trusses and round, shiny green leaves; 'Bernadette' (*R. loranthiflorum* x *R. konori*) with heavily fragrant, fluted and ruffled pink flowers on a compact plant; 'Cyril' (*R. leucogigas* x [*R. konori* x *R. laetum*]) with large pale yellow flowers edged in pink on a tall plant;

Moynier

Peter Sullivan

'Elizabeth Ann Seton' (['Dr. Herman Sleumer' x 'Pink Delight'] x ['Pink Delight' x *R. jasminiflorum*]) with shiny dark green leaves and red buds, veins and midrib that blooms in light pink, flared tubular flowers in a rounded truss; 'Harry Wu' (*R. zoelleri* x *R. leugogigas*) with red buds opening to peach flowers and red-gold tubes and red pedicel and large leaves of a tall plant; 'Humboldt Bay' ('Sir George Holford' x *R. leucogigas*) with fragrant, flared orange-pink flowers and large blue-green leaves on a tall plant; 'Kikori Bay' ([*R. macgregoriae* x *R. zoelleri*] x [*R. laetum* x *R. zoelleri*]) with small bicolor, tubular flowers of yellow-gold and red-orange tubular flowers in a domed truss on a small plant; and 'Lawrence' (*R. lochiae* x *R. pseudonitens*) with hanging bright red, bell-shaped flowers on a graceful plant.

In the San Francisco Bay area in the late 1940s, Maurice and Fran Sumner of San Francisco "discovered" the genus *Rhododendron*, which, in the words of Fran, "took us to England and Scotland, opened castle doors, and took us to the most primitive areas in New Guinea" (Fran Sumner, personal communication). The genus was to become a life-long absorbing hobby. To learn more, they sent for J. B. Stephenson's book on rhododendrons and sent to England for seed. They built a frame for growing on their seedlings, and as plants grew they became more and more excited. When they learned of the American Rhododendron Society, they helped form the California Chapter in 1952, and Maurice was one of the first chapter presidents. But their enthusiasm did not stop there. In the 1960 they became interested in the vireyas and traveled to Papua New Guinea to see these plants in the wild (see Chapter 8).

The Sumners approached hybridizing with equal zeal, creating several outstanding hybrids for California gardeners. Their top prize was 'Mi Amor' (*R. lindleyi* x *R. nuttallii*), a cross of two

Sumner

Maurice and Fran Sumner

species of subsection *Maddenia*—a subsection whose species can tolerate temperatures to about 15°F. The fragrant, bell-shaped, white flowers of 'Mi Amor' are up to 6 inches (15 cm) wide with a yellow throat, with leaves of dark green on top and gray beneath on a tall plant. Besides earning numerous truss show prizes, the plant earned an Award of Merit from the Royal Horticultural Society. Fran chose the Spanish name translated "my love" to honor her husband. 'Martha Wright' (*R. burmanicum* x 'Fragrantissimum'), whose parents include species of subsections *Maddenia* and *Edgeworthia*, bears fragrant flowers of creamy white with yellow centers in flat trusses of four flowers. 'My Lady' ('Forestianum' selfed) bears flowers of white blushed with pink with a pale yellow throat held in open trusses and has glossy, puckered leaves on a compact plant. 'Owen Pearce' ('Saffron Queen' x *R. burmanicum*) opens from dark yellow buds to light yellow flowers in open trusses with a compact plant habit.

The Sumner's garden, Monte Toyon, in Aptos, California, displays the Sumner's hybrids and many large-leaf rhododendrons.

Bob Scott of Kensington, California, on San Francisco Bay, also was drawn to the species of subsection *Maddenia* in his hybridizing; a group of rhododendrons generally too tender for British Columbia, Washington, and Oregon but suited to the northern California climate. Scott, who managed the rhododendron dell at the University of California Botanical Garden in Berkeley, came to appreciate the wonderful attributes of these plants: early bloom, fragrance, elegant flower, interesting foliage, and peeling bark. Wishing to enhance the garden value of this group by imparting compact form along with floriferousness, in the 1960s he first began crossing species outside the group. His 'Pink Snowflakes' (*R. racemosum* x *R. moupinense*) is a semi-dwarf with good plant habit and in Cali-

fornia blooms floriferously in winter with pink and white flowers against glossy, dark green foliage. 'Lemon Mist' (*R. xanthostephanum* x *R. leucaspis*), also a semi-dwarf, bears light yellow flowers and is also floriferous and of good habit. Then Scott introduced Maddenia genes to his program and produced 'Meadowgold' (*R. burmanicum* x 'Lemon Mist'), a low grower with tiny leaves and yellow flowers with spotting on dorsal lobes. He added fragrance in 'Rose Scott' ('Else Frye' x [*R. johnstoneanum* x *R. cubittii*]) with light flowers and dark pink throat in a flat truss. 'Scott's Starbright' ('Else Frye' x *R. dalhousiae* var. *rhabdotum*) has yellow buds striped with red opening to wavy, white, scented flowers with yellow spotting and red stripes on the outside. 'Butterhorn' ('Eldorado' x *R. dalhousiae* var. *rhabdotum*) bears tubular yellow flowers on a low, compact plant. 'Lake Lorraine' (*R. burmanicum* x *R. cuffeanum*) bears large creamy flowers opening from chartreuse buds and has glossy green foliage.

Like many other avid hybridizers, Scott's crosses became more complex, often including his own hybrids. 'Parker Smith' ([*R. johnstoneanum* x *R. cubittii*] x *R. chrysodoron*) bears fragrant, bright yellow flowers and blooms for five months, beginning in December. 'Saffron Meadow' ([*R. burmanicum* x *R. chrysodoron*] x *R. valentinianum*) has dark yellow flowers and darker throat on a mounding plant of medium height with round leaves and bronze hairs. 'Scott's Valentine' ([*R. johnstoneanum* x *R. cubittii*] x [*R. moupinense* x 'Rose Scott']) bears fragrant, bright pink flowers on a spreading semi-dwarf plant with glossy foliage and red new growth and flower bud scales of red, silver, gold, and green. This plant brings together Scott's ambitious goals. Even after Scott became ill with multiple sclerosis, he continued to hybridize, producing still more wonders combining the *Maddenia* species with other lepidote rhododendrons.

Evans

Jack and Fleurette Evans

Numerous others in the San Francisco Bay area have produced plants for this climate. Parker Smith of Sebastopol has been involved in making crosses of the tender Maddenias. Two unregistered crosses are 'Winter Peach' and 'Mary Scanlon'. William Moyles of Oakland has produced 'Fleurette Evans' ('Seta', selfed), 'Winter Lights' ('Bric-a-Brac' x *R. scopulorum*), and also works with vireyas. Allan Korth of Soquel created 'Tahitian Dawn' ('Lem's Cameo' x 'Skipper'). Howard Kerrigan of Hayward is best known for his evergreen azalea crosses, the Kerrigan Hybrid Group, but he also crossed subsection *Maddenia* species. Among these crosses is 'Virginia Stewart' ('Countess of Haddington' x *R. nuttallii*). Jack and Fleurette Evans of Oakland also worked with tender rhododendrons, producing 'Paul Molinari' (*R. veitchianum* x 'Else Frye') and 'Jack Evans' (*R. nuttallii* x *R. nuttallii*). Jack, who served a term as Western Vice-president of the society, named one of his crosses 'Alfred Martin' (*R. edgeworthii* x 'Else Frye') after his good friend. Martin frequently visited Evans on business trips to the West Coast.

Further north, Dr. Paul J. Bowman of Fort Bragg, California, came to northern California in the early 1900s as a physician to the lumber mill employees and most of the town's residents.

He soon became aware of the indigenous rhododendron species—*Rhododendron macrophyllum* and *R. occidentale*—and the suitability of the climate for the common hybrids available at that time. His interest led him to correspond with English growers, sponsor plant hunting expeditions to Asia, and then began his own collection of rhododendrons particularly suited to the coastal northern California climate, particularly the species of subsection *Maddenia*. As his interest grew, he began hybridizing and produced several outstanding plants still available today.

One well-known hybrid dating from 1947 but still available today is 'Ruby Bowman' (*R. fortunei* x 'Lady Bligh'), bearing pink flowers with dark pink throat on a large plant with hardiness of -5°F (-21°C). Bowman's hybridizing interests, however, focused more and more on the subsection *Maddenia*, characterized by flower fragrance and voluptuous bloom. Its relative tenderness allows success in northern California but generally not further north except with winter protection. His most well-known hybrid, 'Else Frye' (*R. ciliicalyx* x unknown), first flowered in 1950. The fragrant flowers of 'Else Frye' are 4 inches (10 cm) wide, white with a blush of pink, yellow in the throat, and born in loose trusses. The leaves are leathery, glossy, and deeply veined on a plant that

Stewart

'Ruby Bowman'

Goheen

'Else Frye'

grows to about 4 feet (1 m) in ten years. It is hardy to 15°F (-10°C). He used 'Else Frye' to produce his 'California Gold' ('Else Frye' x Eldorado Group) with fragrant, bright yellow flowers 3¼ inches (8 cm) wide on a plant that grows about 3 feet (1 m) in ten years, with a hardiness to 15°F (-10°C).

Bowman was known for his hospitality in sharing his garden with visitors and the inspiration he gave to Everett Farwell and others to form the California Chapter of the American Rhododendron Society in 1952. The society awarded him with its Gold Medal in 1968.

John Druecker came to northern California with his wife, Helen, in 1935 to work at the historic Cottage Gardens Nursery in Eureka, later settling in Fort Bragg to start the Druecker Nursery. In spite of the Depression, John and Helen sustained their interest in rhododendron growing, breeding, and exploration. While serving in World War II, Druecker gained notoriety for landscaping the base hospital on the South Pacific island of Tinian with native plant material. After the war, he turned to hybridizing. His hybrids are known for their large flowers. Among those still available are: 'Helen Druecker' (*R. elliottii* x 'Betty Wormald') with large, wide leaves and big pink flowers up to 4½ inches (11 cm) across in trusses of up to sixteen flowers; 'Jim

Philp

Paul and Ruby Bowman in center

Philp

John Druecker

Drewry' ('Ruby F. Bowman' x *R. elliottii*) with funnel-shaped bright red flowers and darker red spots held in large trusses of up to twenty-seven flowers; 'George Ritter' (*R. griersonianum* x unknown) bearing large pink flowers with red throats in lax trusses; 'Stacia' (*R. fortunei* ssp. *fortunei* x 'Everestianum') with large, fragrant, violet flowers and blotch of green; and 'Lucy's Good Pink' ('Ruby F. Bowman' x *R. griersonianum*) with large leaves and dark pink flowers up to 4½ inches (11 cm) wide and red calyx carried in lax trusses.

Philp

'Jim Drewry'

John Druecker was active in the Noyo Chapter of the American Rhododendron Society and the Mendocino Coast Botanical Gardens.

Eleanor and Jim Drewy came to Fort Bragg from southern California in the 1960s and fell in love with rhododendrons after spotting 'Cornubia' in full bloom. They started Trillium Lane Nursery and introduced many of the Druecker and Bowman hybrids to the public. After Jim died, Eleanor married Bruce Philp, and together the Philps continued the Trillium Lane Nursery.

Dr. Richard Anderson of northern California, in 1967 used Bowman's 'Else Frye' as a seed parent crossed with the Maddenia *Rhododendron johnstoneanum* to produce four named hybrids still available: 'Doctor Richard Anderson' with 4¼-inch (11 cm), white blushed pink flowers with an orange blotch on a low-growing plant; 'Humboldt Surprise' with 3¼-inch (8 cm) yellow flowers with a dark yellow blotch on a low-growing plant; 'Quala-A-Wa-Loo' with 3¼-inch (8 cm) yellow flowers with a red blotch and small leaves on a plant that grows about 30 inches (75 cm) in ten years; and 'Super Jay' with 3½-inch (9 cm) white flowers and orange blotch on a plant that also grows about 30 inches in ten years.

Catherine Weeks of Eureka, California, a nursery owner, became interested in rhododendrons in 1966 when she saw Endre Ostbo's 'King of Shrubs' blooming at a friend's house. Once she became acquainted with the variety within the genus, she knew she had to start growing them. Growing on seeds of the cross ('Cynthia' x *R. decorum*) led her to making crosses of her own. Her hybridizing goals have been flower colors different from the parents, better leaves, and fragrance. Among her named crosses are: 'Angel Wings' ('Loderi Pink Diamond' x 'Polar Bear'), 'Arthur Charles' ('Sir Charles Lemon' x

'Gill's Cream'), 'Cindy Ann' (*R. decorum* x ['Mrs. Horace Fogg' x 'Diva']), and 'Kathy Ann Pieries' ('Cynthia' x *R. decorum*).

The British Columbia and California hybridizers, of course, communicated with those of Washington and Oregon, often through the channels provided by the American Rhododendron Society. Together the West Coast hybridizers comprised a lively group of like-minded individuals bent on one purpose—creating the best plants their imaginations could envision.

CHAPTER 8

RHODODENDRON ACTIVITY
IN THE 1990S

Two activities in which West Coast rhododendron enthusiasts are intensely involved today are hybridizing and plant exploration.

The experience of previous rhododendron hybridizers and explorers, together with a growing body of scientific research on rhododendrons, has equipped current hybridizers and explorers with a sophisticated body of knowledge to enhance their interest in creating new hybrids and to increase their understanding of the evolution and distribution of rhododendrons in the wild. Whether professional or amateur, these "rhodophiles" continue the adventure started over a hundred years ago to capitalize on the beauty and penetrate the mysteries of this great genus.

The large number of species now known to exist within the genus *Rhododendron* offers hybridizers a vast pool of genes to combine through sexual reproduction to produce a stunning array of hybrids. In spite of the general sexual incompatibility of lepidote and elepidote rhododendrons, the possibility for creating new hybrid rhododendrons is enormous and continues to motivate professional and amateur hybridizers alike in their search for plants different in appearance or cultural needs from their parents. Since Gregor Mendel (1822-1884) discovered how parent plants pass on their genes to their progeny, further research has revealed that most rhododendrons are diploid and have thirteen pairs of chromosomes, which carry the genes in the nuclei of cells. Researchers have also found that occasionally rhododendrons will have three or more sets of chromosomes in the cell nuclei resulting in polyploidy. Polyploid rhododendrons tend to have larger leaves and flowers, characteristics of interest to hybridizers. The chemical colchicine has been found to induce polyploidy in rhododendrons and is used by some hybridizers.

Scientific research and discovery of new species has also enriched the interests of the rhododendron species enthusiasts, who more than ever are trekking to regions where they can see for themselves rhododendrons growing in the wild. Research in rhododendron DNA, the substance of which genes are made, has enabled scientists to begin to determine the relationships of rhododendron species and their evolutionary history, adding to the work begun by Gregor Mendel. New theories of rhododendron distribution, such as that proposed by Irving and Hebda (1993), also enrich the exploration of rhododendrons in the wild.

Stubbs

Dick Cavender, Mike Oliver, Frank Mossman and Art Stubbs

HYBRIDIZING

Even though the unplanned or random cross of two rhododendrons can produce a beautiful plant, experienced hybridizers urge beginners to plan their crosses to best achieve their desired results. The late David Leach estimated that the time between making a cross and commercial production is about twenty years. If one is to devote this much time to producing a good, commercial hybrid, common sense tells us to make a wise investment and to better the odds in the gamble.

In his book *Rhododendrons of the World*, Leach discusses some basic principles of genetics regarding rhododendron hybridizing—principles that guide hybridizers today. For a start, today's hybridizers, most of whom are amateur rather than professional, know that most rhododendrons have thirteen pairs of chromosomes for a total of twenty-six and that each chromosome carries up to one thousand genes that af-

fect appearance and vigor. Today's knowledgeable hybridizers also know that many genes can influence one characteristic. They also understand how parents pass on dominant and recessive genes to the progeny through the process of meiosis during sexual reproduction. They are well aware of the virtually infinite number of gene combinations possible when they take that first step of dabbing pollen of one rhododendron onto the stigma of another. They understand what Leach was talking about when he wrote: "The multitude of different combinations of the genes in the chromosomes when the pairs are reduced to one in the pollen and in the ovule and then once again combined into pairs in the progeny provides the basis for manipulating the traits of rhododendrons in breeding" (Leach 1961).

Even after the elementary principles of genetics were understood, rhododendron hybridizers discovered other tendencies in the genus. For example, in their search for yellow flowers, they found that yellow pigment, which is controlled by a number of genes, can be hidden in the first generation (F_1) but come out in the second generation (F_2). In breeding for fragrance, they found that it is often "linked" to another characteristic—pastel flower colors. And sterility and incompatibility sometimes caused problems. The West Coast hybridizers learned from each other but to a greater extent learned from preceding hybridizers, and they continue to learn from contemporary hybridizers throughout the world. Instead of repeating primary crosses, they often save time by crossing the early hybrids with parents of good species forms or crossing later hybrids that carry genes from a variety of species or, in the case of Warren Berg, use species not often used in hybridizing. The seed and pollen exchanges of the American Rhododendron Society and its chapters and informal exchanges among individuals have expedited the hybridizing efforts. The result is that many of today's hybrids carry an extremely complicated parentage.

Berg

'Queen Bee'

As an example of the contemporary West Coast hybridizing efforts, a group of hybridizers has been chosen for discussion to illustrate their methods and achievements and to show the importance of close contact with other hybridizers (they participate in the Northwest Hybridizers Study Group affiliated with the American Rhododendron Society). Most of these hybridizers began their work in earlier years and could rightfully have been discussed in chapters 6 and 7, but since their work continues to this day, they have been chosen to show the direction of current rhododendron hybridizing.

Warren Berg of Port Ludlow, Washington, a retired World War II navy dive-bomber pilot and commercial airline pilot, became interested in rhododendrons as a child, influenced by his mother's collection. In the 1960s he became involved in propagation, learning from the Northwest's greats—Ben Nelson, Hjalmar Larson, Lester Brandt, William Whitney, and Ben Lancaster—and Dr. Marc Cathey of the National Arboretum in Washington D.C. He experimented with air rooting, lighting, hormones, and misting in a greenhouse and began his crosses with the Exbury form of *Rhododendron degronianum* ssp. *yakushimanum* to produce hardy hybrids with indumented foliage. In 1966,

Berg

Warren Berg

Berg

'Wanna Bee'

Berg

'Jan Bee'

he made the cross that would produce the out-standing foliage plant 'Golfer' (*R. degronianum* ssp. *yakushimanum* x *R. pseudochrysanthum*) with "yak"-shaped leaves that carry indumentum on tops and undersides of the leaves all year long. Although there were some successes, he admits he made the mistake of not continuing with the next generation. Instead, he abandoned this project and began striving for a good yellow, one of which was 'Berg's Yellow' ('Mrs. Betty Robertson' x 'Fred Rose').

When Berg realized that he lacked space to accommodate this group of hybrids, in the 1970s he opted for a hybridizing program that would produce lepidotes with small, compact form, indumented foliage, and a profusion of flowers. He made primary crosses of superior forms of dwarf species that had not been much used before on the West Coast. One superior parent was the yellow-flowering, prostrate *R. keiskei* var. *cordifolia*, which he introduced to the United States from Japan. 'Yaku Fairy' is a named clone of this variety. Among the progeny are some of the most successful hybrids produced on the West Coast. 'Patty Bee' (*R. keiskei* 'Yaku Fairy' x *R. fletcherianum*), named for his wife Patty, won the Superior Plant Award from the American Rhododendron Society in 1985. This dense, ground-hugging plant with small leaves bears

clear yellow 2-inch (5 cm) flowers and is tolerant of heat and sun. Another true winner is the taller 'Ginny Gee' (*R. keiskei* prostrate form x *R. racemosum*) with small leaves and 1-inch (2.5 cm) flowers of pink dappled with white that bloom at branch ends. This hybrid also won the Superior Plant Award in 1985. Another success using *R. keiskei* is 'Golden Bee' (*R. keiskei* 'Yaku Fairy' x *R. melinanthum* now *R. mekongense*) with a broad form up to 2 feet (0.5 m) and yellow flowers. Using the cross (*R. campylogynum* 'Patricia' x *R. keiskei* 'Yaku Fairy') Berg created three more winners in the dwarf category: 'Too Bee', 'Wee Bee', and 'Not Too Bee'. 'Too Bee' has pink flowers with dark pink spotting on a broad, rounded plant. 'Wee Bee' and 'Not Too Bee' have funnel-shaped flowers of red shading to pink in the throat with red rays on each lobe.

Holding to his goal of dwarf plants with good foliage, Berg has in recent years extended his hybridizing with the species *R. proteoides*, aiming for a hardy rock garden plant with star foliage and a full-trussed flower of good color.

Berg has been active in the American Rhododendron Society for many years, receiving its Gold Medal in 1989. He has received recognition in Germany for his hybrids and has actively served the Rhododendron Species Foundation. He is recognized for his generous plant

Watson

Elsie Watson

and bronze spotting in a rounded truss on a smaller plant than 'Blue Boy'. Using Lem's 'Anna', she produced 'Katrina' ('Anna' x 'Purple Splendour') bearing red-violet flowers with a black blotch. A sister seedling, 'Marley Hedges', bears white flowers with red-violet margins and flower backsides and violet blotches. In her many years of hybridizing Watson has achieved goals of fragrance and early bloom. Her current goal is to produce a violet-flowering rhododendron with a large calyx.

Dr. Edwin Brockenbrough of Seattle made his first named crosses in the early 1970s. His hybrids are known for their voluptuous flowers in blends of colors. He frequently used *Rhododendron degronianum* ssp. *yakushimanum* to impart good form and foliage and built upon other West Coast hybrids, such as 'Lem's Cameo', 'Brandt's Tropicana', and 'Hotei' to produce his uniquely beautiful plants. 'Apricot Fantasy' ('Hotei' x 'Brandt's Tropicana') bears bi-colored flowers of orange and yellow with red spotting and a double calyx on a dense, spreading plant. 'Bambino' (['Britannia' x ssp. *yakushimanum*] x 'Lem's Cameo') bears bi-colored flowers of peach and yellow spotted with red on the upper petals and red in the center and with a large calyx. Dark green foliage is textured and dense on this low growing

donations and willingness to share his experience through talks and participation in study groups. His plant explorations in Asia are legend and will be discussed later in this chapter.

Elsie Watson of Kirkland, Washington, has been hybridizing for over thirty-five years and is especially known for her violet-flowering creations. Of the approximately 500 crosses she has made, she has registered the names of less than ten, a tribute to her ruthless culling of inferior plants. Among her successes is 'Blue Boy' ('Blue Ensign' x 'Purple Splendour'), a cross made in 1965 bearing wavy-edged, blue-violet flowers and black blotch in tight trusses on a well-shaped plant growing to about 5 feet (1.5 m) in ten years. 'Blue Hawaii' of the same parentage bears dark violet flowers with a green blotch

Watson

'Blue Boy'

Brockenbrough

**Dr. Edwin (Ned) Brockenbrough
with his wife, Jean**

plant. 'Horizon Dawn' (['Hotei' x 'Brandt's Tropicana'] x [ssp. *yakushimanum* x ('Alice Franklin' x 'Virginia Scott')]) bears light yellow flowers with bright yellow throats on a compact, rounded plant with bright green leaves. 'Horizon Lakeside' (['Nancy Evans' x 'Lem's Cameo'] x 'Skipper') bears fragrant, large, pale yellow flowers with a red throat in ball trusses on a compact, low growing plant. His outstanding 'Horizon Monarch' ('Nancy Evans' x 'Point Defiance', a tetraploid) bears large trusses of yellow-green

flowers of heavy substance with a red flare, opening from red buds and with large, leathery leaves. Perhaps his best-known cross is 'Nancy Evans' ('Hotei' x 'Lem's Cameo'), whose flowers change in color as they mature, beginning with orange-red buds, opening to orange-yellow, and changing to golden yellow. It has a large calyx and low growing, compact form. His 'Paprika Spiced' ('Hotei' x 'Brandt's Tropicana') bears pale yellow flowers dotted with paprika-red spots with pink on the backside of the upper lobe—a most unusual color pattern. 'Pineapple Delight' of the same parentage has funnel-shape yellow flowers tempered by a creamy sheen in rounded trusses on a plant of rounded form with dark green leaves.

Brockenbrough has been able to bring together extraordinary flower color and plants of good form and foliage, building upon the achievements of previous hybridizers and his own hybridizing genius. He currently is particularly interested in using tetraploid rhododendrons in his breeding program. He received the Silver Medal from the American Rhododendron Society in 1985.

Frank Fujioka of Whidbey Island, Washington, began hybridizing after visits to Halfdan Lem, who inspired him through the "magic he could create" (Bell 1997).

Goheen

'Paprika Spiced'

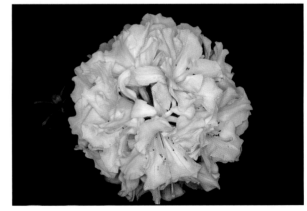

Greer

'Bambino'

Fujioka recalls his first meeting with Lem. "I went there and, as I parked the car, I saw thousands of large plants that appeared to be rhodies, but I had never seen such large ones. I asked the man for a 'Jean Marie' and he said he didn't have those but he had many 'finer plants'. That man was Halfdan Lem! He had just finished his afternoon nap and was very enthusiastic about showing me different rhododendrons. It was one of the most enjoyable and significant afternoons of my life" (Fujioka, personal communication).

Fujioka visited Lem regularly, witnessing Lem's habit of using tobacco spit on flower stigmas to prepare them to receive the pollen. When he saw Lem in his 80s in ill health and walking with a cane but still putting pollen on flowers, Fujioka realized how long-term goals could prolong and enrich one's life. He decided how he was going to spend his retirement—hybridizing rhododendrons. Fujioka was also led to Jim and Betty Caperci, who educated him in the lepidotes, and to Lester Brandt, who along with Lem aroused his interest in hybridizing.

From the beginning, in the 1960s, his primary interests were good foliage and form. His first named hybrid was a lepidote cross made in 1966, 'Vibrant Violet' (*R. impeditum* x *R. augustinii* 'Tower Court'), with small, pointed, dark green leaves on a plant that grows approximately 3 feet (1 m) in ten years. Its flowers are a bright violet. In the mid 1960s he acquired a plant of *R. degronianum* ssp. *yakushimanum* 'Koichiro Wada', which became his greatest treasure. From it he produced 'Silver Skies' (*R. degronianum* ssp. *yakushimanum* 'Koichiro Wada' x Medusa Group). He began looking for "yak" hybrids and found 'Yaku Sunrise', 'Yaku Incense', and 'Noyo Brave', which became the basis of his hybridizing efforts. He then began using *R. bureavii*, *R. rex*, and *R. macabeanum* hybrids and 'Noyo Chief', aiming for darker colors and good foliage.

Fujioka

Frank Fujioka

Fujioka culls his seedlings mercilessly and has named very few of his crosses. But among those named are 'Elsie Watson' ('Anna' x 'Purple Lace'), an upright growing plant attaining about 5 feet (1.5 m) in ten years and bearing light violet-pink flowers with a dark violet star in the throat and violet spots on the upper lobe, and 'Cranberry Lace' of the same cross. 'Midnight Mystique' ('Midnight' x 'One Thousand Butterflies') bears flowers of red-violet with a prominent white star in the center. 'Starbright Champagne' (['Yaku Sunrise' x 'Hansel'] x 'Lem's Cameo') bears champagne colored flowers vaguely shaped like lilies on a well-formed plant. 'Primary Pink' (['Yaku Sunrise' x ('C.I.S.' x 'Jingle Bells')] x 'Lem's Cameo') also bears pastel flowers but in a light pink.

Fujioka also works closely with East Coast hybridizers, some of who make an annual trip to his garden for pollen. Like many other West Coast hybridizers, he has become aware of the need for cold tolerance in less rhododendron-friendly climates and has added heat and drought tolerance to his list of hybridizing goals, along with unusual flower petals.

Fujioka is active in the Whidbey Island Chapter of the American Rhododendron Society and generously gives talks on his hybridizing all over the country.

Pat Halligan, also of Whidbey Island, is a dentist by profession but holds a doctoral degree in plant ecology. Although his interest in plants goes back to childhood, his interest in rhododendrons began in 1980 when he moved to the Northwest. From the beginning he laid out specific hybridizing goals—goals both unique and difficult. First was to produce Maddenia-like fragrance in rhododendrons hardy in the Northwest. Second was to produce a red flowering lepidote. The first goal has eluded him, he admits, but he continues to make crosses with this goal in mind. The second goal has yielded some successes, among them the recently named 'Firecracker Marcia' ([*R. keiskei* var. *cordifolium* x *R. spinuliferum*] x

Halligan

Pat Halligan with 'Pink Prelude'

[(['Mary Fleming' x *R. spinuliferum*] x [*R. racemosum* x *R. spinuliferum*) x (*R. keiskei* x *R. spinuliferum*]). This cross bears flowers with dark pink on the upper side of the petals and red on the back side. Another success came with the cross ([(*R. campylogynum* x *R. spinuliferum*) x near sibling 'Firecracker Denisial'] x 'Firecracker Tori') that bears flowers of dark red on both the upper and back side of the petals. Halligan has relied on the species *Rhododendron spinuliferum*, which can flower in pink, orange, peach-red, brick-red, or crimson, but also uses *R. calostrotum* 'Gigha', *R. campylogynum*, *R. racemosum*, and *R. keiskei*. "I use every acceptable plant as a parent, rather than selecting the very best and using it alone. I call it 'population breeding' and use it to ensure that unseen genetic material is not lost," Halligan said (Halligan 1997). He found that looking at the flowers of his crosses under fluorescent lights he could see all the "bad" colors—the muddying blues. He decided that he could also screen potential parents by looking at their flowers under fluorescent light where they exhibited their unwanted colors more clearly. Besides the difficulty in getting red flowering plants, he also is faced with the problem of getting a good plant form. But Halligan is not discouraged and continues pursuing his goal in "lonely splendor" with the perspective of the die-hard hybridizer who knows success takes time.

Pat Halligan is active in the American Rhododendron Society, especially on its Meerkerk Rhododendron Gardens Ratings Committee.

James Barlup of Bellevue, Washington, became interested in hybridizing in 1975, making do with the small space afforded by his city lot. From the start, he set specific goals, apricot, orange, and peach flower color, later modifying them to include hardiness to withstand East

Judy Barlup

Jim Barlup

Coast winters. His 'Amber Touch' ('Nadia' x ['Brinny' x Whitney's late frilled yellow]) prolifically bears peach flowers with dark pink rays on a plant of good form growing to 3 feet (1 m) in 10 years and hardy to at least 0°F (-18°C). His 'Coral Mist' ('Nancy Evans' x 'Mrs. Furnivall') has frilly flowers that open from a red bud to pale yellow-pink flowers on the upper side and violet pink on the back side with a border of violet-pink and a yellow blotch with red speckles. It grows to 3 feet (1 m) in 10 years and is hardy to at least 0°F (-18°C).

Barlup has contributed a series of articles on hybridizing to the *Journal American Rhododendron Society* and lectures on the subject of hybridizing.

The goal of the hybridizing partnership of John Winberg of Fall City, Washington, and Clint Smith of Sumner, Washington, first was a big truss, but the goal has broadened to include compact plant habit and hardiness. They also have realized the need for a new, compact, white-flowering rhododendron. With this in mind they produced 'Head Honcho' (*R. degronianum* ssp. *yakushimanum* 'Siouxon' x 'Mrs. J. G. Millais').

Lloyd and Edna Newcomb of Snohomish, Washington, were influenced by Halfdan Lem early in their hybridizing career. However, one of Lem's suggestions they did *not* follow—throwing out their 'Van Nes Sensation' seedlings because no one would want those colors. Lem said they should be hybridizing for yellows and oranges. One of those seedlings turned out to be their 'Mount Clearview' ('Van Nes Sensation' x 'Purple Splendour'), a real winner with violet flowers on a rounded plant. Their hybridizing goals evolved to include good form and foliage and hardiness. Among their named crosses are: 'Newcomb's Sweetheart' ('Pink Walloper' x *R. decorum*), a broad plant that bears fragrant pink flowers edged in purple; 'Blue Thunder' (open pollinated 'Blue Diamond'), a low grower with violet flowers and foliage that turns dark red in winter; and 'Pridenjoy' ('Lem's Cameo' x 'Kubla Khan') with yellow flowers opening from red buds and with bright green foliage.

In 1968, Dr. Wilbur Anderson began his research on the micropropagation of rhododendrons at the Northwestern Washington Research and Extension Center in Mount Vernon, Washington. The method, known as "tissue culture," is the propagation of plants on an artificial medium under germ-free conditions from small pieces of plant. The method offers the advantage of producing plants more quickly than the classic method of growing on

Cascade Photograhics

Bruce Briggs

The development of the tissue culture method of propagation meant that commercially appealing new hybrids from amateur hybridizers could be propagated and put on the market more quickly. Such has been the case with a number of West Coast hybrids, including Edwin Brockenbrough's 'Nancy Evans', Frank Fujioka's 'Midnight Mystique', Paul Christianson's 'Coral Pacific', and Jim Barlup's 'Coral Mist'. The Briggs Nursery also has been an innovator in the production of tetraploid rhododendrons. In 1997, the nursery registered the name of a tetraploid version of 'Nova Zembla' that had been treated with colchicine, naming the new plant 'Supernova'. The heavily textured flowers are 3½ inches (9 cm) wide in trusses 5½ inches (14 cm) high and wide.

cuttings. Nurserymen Bruce Briggs of Olympia, Washington, Les Clay of Langley, British Columbia, and Bob Hart of Mount Vernon, Washington, joined Anderson in setting up a laboratory in the Briggs Nursery kitchen on the weekends. By 1985, the Briggs Nursery constructed a modern tissue culture laboratory that can produce several million plants a year. The Clay Nursery also built a laboratory and uses tissue culture in its propagation of rhododendrons. Both Bruce Briggs and Les Clay have been active in the American Rhododendron Society for many years and have been true ambassadors for the genus. Bruce Briggs received the Gold Medal from the society in 1994.

Clay

Les Clay

Current West Coast hybridizers continue to build on the vast array of rhododendrons developed previously, creating different and better plants for today's gardens. Although they tend to set more specific goals, they also respect the values instilled by previous hybridizers—patience and close communication with those caught up in the hybridizing gamble.

EXPLORATION IN THE WILD

Coming full circle, many "rhodophiles" are returning to the regions where rhododendrons grow in the wild and where the first rhododendron plant hunters made the discoveries that so transformed gardens of the nineteenth and twentieth centuries.

While the excitement of seeing their favorite shrubs, or parents of these shrubs, growing in pristine environments has particular allure today, some of the early West Coast rhododendron growers also were drawn to original sources in western China, the Himalayas, Japan, and the West Coast itself. Mary Greig of Vancouver Island visited Nepal and Kashmir in 1968. Frank Doleshy of Seattle examined the native *Rhododendron macrophyllum* on Hood Canal in Washington in the early 1960s, observed *R. makinoi*, *R. degronianum*, *R. brachycarpum*, and *R. keiskei* in Japan in 1965 and returned again in 1967 and 1969. In the 1970s he again revisited Japan and also Malaysia's Mt. Kinabalu in search of vireyas. Maurice and Fran Sumner of San Francisco were among the first amateur collectors of vireyas in New Guinea in the early 1960s. In 1970,

Britt Smith of Kent, Washington, established a historic link to Sikkim and the conservation-minded rhododendron enthusiasts of that Himalayan state. In 1974 he organized a trek through its rhododendron country for members of the American Rhododendron Society and the Rhododendron Species Foundation, including Clive Justice of Vancouver, British Columbia, and Dr. Forrest Bump of Forest Grove, Oregon. Through the efforts of Clive Justice the J.D. Hooker Chapter of the American Rhododendron Society was formed.

Leonard Frisbie began the search for the West Coast native azalea *Rhododendron occidentale* in Oregon and California in earnest in the 1950s. He documented its distribution and variation in detail. In the 1960s, Dr. Frank Mossman of Vancouver, Washington, and Britt Smith of Kent, Washington, took up the banner and began a series of explorations that resulted in the selection of superior forms representing a wide variety of flower color in this lovely, fragrant native. Inspired by the Smith-Mossman explorations, Michael McCullough of San Jose, California, began his intensive search in California, finding the azalea growing as far south as San Diego County. Named *R. occidentale* forms include 'Leonard Frisbie', 'Pistol Pete', 'Mini Skirts', 'Rogue River Bell', and 'Stagecoach Cream'.

The number of early West Coast rhododendron aficionados who took to the wilds to see for themselves these plants in their homeland is too long to list. However, the satisfaction they experienced and the stories they told have motivated the current West Coast explorers of the 1990s.

Among explorers of the 1990s is Warren Berg of Port Ludlow, Washington, who made his fifth excursion to China in 1990. (In his 1989 expedition to Yunnan Province, China, he had among his party two other avid West Coast explorers, Gwen Bell of Seattle and June Sinclair of Port Ludlow, Washington). His search for *Rhododendron proteoides*, a species he uses in his hybridizing program, adds a special focus to this expedition. In 1991, he followed in the steps of Frank Kingdon-Ward through Muli in the southwest corner of Sichuan, China. In 1992, his most recent trip, he returned to western China and explored the Mekong Salween Divide together with Scottish explorer Peter Cox. His written accounts and stunning photographs document his finds and adventures in articles in the *Journal American Rhododendron Society*.

The native regions of the vireya rhododendrons continue to hold interest for West Coast explorers in the 1990s. Clive Justice explored areas of Malaysia while advising the park department of the city of Kuala Lumpur on landscaping. During his frequent trips to that country he observed many vireyas in the wild. In 1991, Clarice Clark visited the Malaysian state of Sabah in search of vireyas in the wild. (Clark had also been a member of the 1990 Warren Berg expedition to China.) Although the trip was designed as a "soft adventure" rather than an expedition, she saw a good selection of vireya species on Mt. Kinabalu.

In 1998, Hank Helm of Bainbridge Island, Washington, and John Farbarik of Silverdale, Washington, explored on the island of Sulawesi in Indonesia for vireya rhododendrons. This expedition of two, with the help of a guide, found approximately fifteen vireya species in this relatively unexplored rhododendron region. In 1998, Helm also traveled to Yunnan, China, in a party of fourteen, including Dr. Benjamin Hall, a botanist from the University of Washington, and Dr. Amy Denton, a plant geneticist from Washington.

Chip Muller of Seattle visited Sikkim in 1992 with a party of nineteen, including his sister, Sue Muller Hacking, of Redmond, Washington. Their father, George Muller, had explored the region during World War II. Chip Muller had accompanied Warren Berg on his 1986 exploration to southeastern Tibet. Then in 1995, he, along with his friend Keith White of Salem, Oregon, explored in southeastern Tibet, making the arduous trek over the Doshong La. Near the pass they found an "unforgettable" alpine meadow of numerous alpine rhododendrons and companions and over the pass in the province of Pemako many other rhododendron riches. In 1997, Keith White and Bob Zimmermann of Port Ludlow, Washington, explored Tibet deep in its southeast corner in search of rhododendrons.

One of the most avid of the current explorers is Steve Hootman, curator of the Rhododendrons Species Botanical Garden in Federal Way, Washington. He accompanied Peter Cox on his 1995 expedition to the Sichuan and Yunnan provinces of China, impressing Cox with his enthusiasm. Hootman again accompanied Cox on an expedition to the Salween Valley in Yunnan, China, in 1997–

Justice

Clive Justice

an area known for its high rainfall that lived up to its reputation. Then in 1998, Hootman again joined Cox on an expedition to Tibet and experienced the not uncommon change of route because of political unrest.

Although Asia beckons to the adventurous spirit of many "rhodophiles" today, the natives at home on the West Coast also continue to have their appeal. Dennis Hendrickson of Renton, Washington, searches for the deciduous *Rhododendron albiflorum* on the cool, north and west facing subalpine slopes of the Cascade and Olympic mountain ranges. Members of the Willamette Chapter of the American Rhododendron Society travel annually to the Siskiyou Mountains of southwest Oregon to see *R. occidentale* blooming in the spring. A project sponsored by the Rhododendron Species Foundation, named the Western North American Rhododendron Species Project, is yet another indication of the interest in indigenous rhododendrons of the West Coast. Its goal is to collect and store in one location all known information about the native *Rhododendron* species of western United States and Canada. Involved in the project are Hank Helm, Bob Zimmermann, John Farbarik, Clarice Clark, George Ryan, Steve Hootman, and Rick Peterson.

The observation of rhododendron species in the wild has led to a keen interest in the variation *within* a species, whereas in times past the focus was finding the best forms of a species. Recent scientific research into rhododendron DNA has also piqued an interest among amateurs in the evolutionary history of this 60 million-year-old genus.

Among both the West Coast rhododendron hybridizers and explorers, the fervor for new creations and discoveries remains intact. And, as always, the amateur and professional, the neophyte and experienced, dive into the milieu together to pursue their shared interest in this magnificent genus.

APPENDIX I

CHARTER MEMBERS OF THE AMERICAN RHODODENDRON SOCIETY

(*The Rhododendron Yearbook For 1946*, Portland, OR: American Rhododendron Society)

Adair, Chas. S., Medford, OR
Arelt, Eugene, Baldwin, NY
Bacher, John G., Portland, OR
Baldwin, Neil, Portland, OR
Baltz, E. P., Gresham, OR
Baumer, John, Northport, NY
Bentelle, W. E., Portland, OR
Bergen, Mrs. John, Coos Bay, OR
Berry, Mrs. A. C. U., Portland, OR
Blake, Mrs. Anson S., Berkeley, CA
Bowen, J. Herbert, Tacoma, WA
Bowers, Clement Gray, Main, NY
Bowman, Dr. Paul Jay, Fort Bragg, CA
Brandt, Lester E., Puyallup, WA
Brennen, James J., Edmonds, WA
Brydon, P. H., Granger, WA
Buckley, E. N., Olympia, WA
Burnaugh, S. L., Portland, OR
Burtis, Herbert S., Seattle, WA
Butler, Mrs. Dorothy, Portland, OR
Chapman, Mrs. W. F., Roseburg, OR
Churchill, Vernon R., Portland, OR
Clark, Gordon, Eugene, OR

Cobb, Forest, Portland, OR
Collins, Dean, Portland, OR
Combs, Mrs. A. B., Portland, OR
Creed, E. Victor, Portland, OR
Crocker, L. P., Medford, OR
Cushman, Mrs. E. A., Tigard, OR
Cushman, E. A., Tigard, OR
DeClements, Mrs., R. C., Bremerton, WA
DeClements, R. C., Bremerton, WA
Drese, Otto, Baldwin, NY
Eddie, H. M., Sardis, BC
Eggerman, D. G., Seattle, WA
English, Carl, Seattle, WA
Esch, Bernard J., Portland, OR
Esch, Mrs. Florence, Portland, OR
Fahey, Philip B., Seattle, WA
Farrill, Ed, Salem, OR
Foland, Milton A., Portland, OR
Frazier, Mrs. Kathryn, Woodland, WA
Gainer, Russel, Newberg, OR
Gaines, Melva A., Portland, OR
Gault, Pem, Portland, OR
Gick, Dr. Royal, Eugene, OR

Gill, Raymond, Portland, OR
Glass, Powell, Lynchburg, VA
Goodman, Dr. George, Portland, OR
Grace, George D., Portland, OR
Graham, Mrs. Donald G., Seattle, WA
Graham, Lt. Col. Donald G., Seattle, WA
Greene, William A., Seattle, WA
Greig, E. & M., Royston, BC, Canada
Griffith, David, Portland, OR
Griswold, Mrs. Walter, S., Bellevue, WA
Gustafson, A., Portland, OR
Haddon, Dr. J. E., Bremerton, WA
Hammerly, Hugh, Albany, OR
Handley, John H., Seattle, WA
Hansen, Mrs. Ruth Martin, Portland, OR
Hardgrove, Donald L., Baldwin, NY
Harding, Mrs. A. H., Portland, OR
Harms, H. H., Portland, OR
Harris, Dr. Arthur K., Camas, WA
Hart, John J., Sayville, NY
Hart, Mrs. Philip, Portland, OR
Hennessey, Roy, Hillsboro, OR
Henny, John, Brooks, OR
Henny, Rudolph, Brooks, OR
Hicks Nursery, Westbury, NY
Hill, V. D., Salem, OR
Holmdahl, O. E., Seattle, WA
Horr, Neal L., Portland, OR
Imbler, Ray M., Portland, OR
Iufer, Ernest, Salem, OR
James, C.A., Tacoma, WA
James, D. W., Eugene, OR
Jaquith, Walter L., Newberg, OR
Johnson, Mrs. Joe M., Portland, OR
Johnson, Joe M., Portland, OR
Johnson, Lewis, Portland, OR
Jufer, Ernest, Salem, OR
Kamp, Aloyo Weeme, Brooks, OR
Kausen, Otto, Eureka, CA
Klager, F. L., Woodland, WA
Ladd, Orval S., Portland, OR
Lancaster, B. F., Camas, WA
Larson, H. L., Tacoma, WA
Layritz, Richard, Victoria, BC Canada
Lee, Frederic, Bethesda, MD

Lincoln, Irving B., Portland, OR
Lipscomb, Dr. E. D., Portland, OR
Livingston, Earl G., Everett, WA
Lynch, Mrs. Matthew J., Portland, OR
Lyons, M. W., Eugene, OR
Malmo, Mrs. Clark B., Seattle, WA
McDonald, C. L., Salem, OR
McLean, Arthur M., Portland, OR
McMahan, Theresa S., Mercer Island, WA
Mehrens, H. Klaus, Elmhurst, IL
Menke, W., Portland, OR
Mills, Mrs. R. W., Woodland, WA
Mitsch, Grant E., Canby, OR
Moffenbier, Clarence, Salem, OR
Mulder, John, Milwaukie, OR
Myhre, Clifford, W., Tacoma, WA
Nearing, G. G., Ridgewood, NJ
Nelson, B. F., Snohomish, WA
Nielsen, Fred A., Seattle, WA
Ostbo, Endre, Bellevue, WA
Otten, George, Portland, OR
Parker, Gerald, Portland, OR
Parker, Howard, Portland, OR
Parker, Wm., Portland, OR
Pearcy, Harry L., Salem, OR
Peffer, Rex, Salem, OR
Perry, Geo. H., Corbett, OR
Peterson, E. R., Portland, OR
Phetteplace, Dr. Carl H., Eugene, OR
Radovich, Nikolas, G., Portland, OR
Richards, Anne, Mount Vernon, WA
Ridgway, C. E., Kirkland, WA
Roberts, James N., Portland, OR
Robinson, William, Portland, OR
Rosefield, Reno, Tigard, OR
Runstetler, N. E., Kirkland, WA
Saunders, Merle F., Eugene, OR
Savage, Glenn N., Portland, OR
Schaefer, John W., Olympia, WA
Schedler, Miss Bertha, Portland, OR
Schedler, Miss Elsie, Portland, OR
Schonwald, Mrs. Philipp, Seattle, WA
Schutt, Dr. Ray L., Bremerton, WA
Seabrook, C. Courtney, Bridgeton, NJ
Searle, J. D., Chehalis, WA

Seevers, Harry V., Ottawa, KS
Senko, J. F., Cornelius, OR
Silvester, Richard, Washington, DC
Simons, Jack, Eugene, OR
Speybrock, Frank, Gresham, OR
Steinmetz, A. H., Portland, OR
Stockdale, Mrs. L. O., Portland, OR
Taylor, Shelton M., Portland, OR
Tomasello, Nick, Seattle, WA
Tucker, W. G., Portland, OR
Turner, Mrs. Ada V. H., Waldport, OR
Van Allen, Paul E., Portland, OR

Van Veen, Theodore, Portland, OR
Voinot, Mrs. Paul, Bellevue, WA
Vollum, C. A., Portland, OR
Walker, Dr. J. Douglas, Chehalis, WA
Walker, Robert A., Portland, OR
Warnock, Sada, Portland, OR
Weinert, W. W., Brooks, OR
White, Lewis M., Portland, OR
Whitney, W. E., Camas, WA
Wright, Arthur C., Milwaukie, OR
Zenor, John L., Agate Beach, OR

APPENDIX II

WEST COAST HYBRIDIZERS

Anderson, Edwin, T.
Anderson, Richard
Arneson, Ivan and Robertha
Bacher, John G.
Barlup, James
Barto, James
Beck, Mrs. Howard
Berg, Warren
Bovee, Robert
Bowman, Paul J.
Brandt, Lester
Brockenbrough, Edwin
Brydon, P. H.
Bump, Dr. Forrest
Caperci, James
Childers, Arthur and Maxine
Clark, Roy
Clarke, George W.
Davis, Joe
Dobbs, Olin O.
Domoto, Toichi
Druecker, John
Elliott, James

Elliott, Walter
Evans, Jack and Fleurette
Finley, Gordon and Vern
Fraser, George
Freimann, LaVern
Frisbie, Leonard
Fujioka, Frank
Goheen, David
Grace, George D.
Greer, Edgar
Greer, Harold
Greig, Ted and Mary
Griswold, Garda
Guttormsen, Bill
Halligan, Pat
Henny, John
Henny, Rudolph
Holden, John
Holland, Stuart
James, Del and Ray
Kerrigan, Howard
Korth, Allan
Kruschke, Franz

Lancaster, Ben
Larson, Hjalmar
Laxdall, Sigrid
Lem, Halfdan
Lofthouse, John
Lyons, Marshall
Manenica, Alma
Mauritsen, Richard
McKee, Dr. C. S.
Minch, Fred
Mossman, Frank
Moyles, William
Moynier, William
Nelson, Ben
Newcomb, Loyd and Edna
Nuccio, Jim
Nuccio, Joe
Nuccio, Julius., Jr.
Nuccio, Julius, Sr.
Nuccio, Tom
Ostbo, Endre
Pearce, Reginald A.
Peste, Fred
Phetteplace, Carl
Rhodes, Robert
Sanders, Merle
Schick, Peter

Scott, Bob
Seabrook, Cecil
Slonecker, Howard
Smith, Britt
Smith, Cecil
Smith, Clint
Smith, Parker
Spady, Herbert
Stephens, J. Freeman
Stockman, Harold and Morna
Sullivan, Peter
Sumner, Maurice
Thompson, Willard and Margaret
Ticknor, Robert
Van Veen, Ted
Van Veen, Theodore, Sr.
Watson, Elsie
Weber, Edwin
Weeks, Catherine
Weesjes, Evelyn Jack
Whitney, William
Wildfong, Milton
Winberg, John
Wright, Arthur A.
Wright, Arthur O.
Wyatt, Vernon
Wyrens, Rollin

APPENDIX III

WEST COAST HYBRIDS

APPENDIX IV

INDEX OF PHOTOGRAPHS

BIBLIOGRAPHY

Arneson, Ivan and Robertha and Adele Jones. 1992. Hybridizing for superior and unique azaleas. *Journal American Rhododendron Society* 49:2-5.

ARS Charter Members. 1995. *Journal American Rhododendron Society* 49:80-82.

ARS Committee on Nomenclature and Registration. 1949. Report of Committee on Nomenclature and Registration. *Quarterly Bulletin of the American Rhododendron Society* 3(4): 8-10.

American Rhododendron Society. 1987. *Plant Awards Program.*

Bacher, John. 1946. America's first rhododendron show. In *The Rhododendron Yearbook for 1946*, Portland, OR: American Rhododendron Society. 1-6.

Bacher, John. 1951. The initial progress of the ARS trial garden. *Quarterly Bulletin of the American Rhododendron Society* 5:14-16.

Bacher, John. 1953. The initial progress of the A.R.S. rock garden. *Quarterly Bulletin of the American Rhododendron Society* 7:41-43.

Badger, Bob, and Ernest Dzurick. 1987. James Francis Caperci. *Journal American Rhododendron Society* 41:162.

Barrett, Clarence. 1994. *History of the Rhododendron Species Foundation, Genesis of a Botanical Garden.* Eugene, OR: Positive Attitudes.

Barrett, Clarence. 1997. *Rhododendrons of the Pacific Northwest: History, Growers, Gardens.* Unpublished manuscript.

Bell, Gwen. 1990. Red hills, limestone mountains and Yunnan rhododendrons. *Journal American Rhododendron Society* 44:62-70.

Bell, Gwen. 1997. Washington hybridizers create plants for the future. *Journal American Rhododendron Society* 51:62-69,119.

Berg, Warren. 1991. British-American Sichuan expedition, 1990. *Journal American Rhododendron Society* 45:62-65, 101-104.

Berg, Warren. 1991. In the steps of Kingdon-Ward through Muli. *Journal American Rhododendron Society* 45:206-213.

Berg, Warren. 1993. Plant hunting near the Mekong Salween Divide. *Journal American Rhododendron Society* 47:62-67.

Boddy, Robert. 1989. John Druecker. *Journal American Rhododendron Society* 43:91-92.

Brydon, P. H. Rhododendron Culture in Great Britain. In *The Rhododendron Yearbook for 1945*, Ed. Dean Collins. Portland, OR: American Rhododendron Society. 1-7.

Capon, Brian. 1990. *Botany for Gardeners*. Portland, OR: Timber Press.

Chamberlain, David, Roger Hyam, George Argent, Gillian Fairweather, Kerry S. Walter. 1996. *The Genus Rhododendron: Its Classification & Synonymy*. Edinburgh: Royal Botanic Garden Edinburgh.

Clark, Clarice. 1999. Mapping *Rhododendron macrophyllum* in the Wind River area of Washington State. *Journal American Rhododendron Society* 53:99-104.

Collins, Dean, ed. 1945. *The Rhododendron Yearbook for 1945*. Portland, OR: American Rhododendron Society.

Cox, Peter. 1995. Plant hunting in Yunnan, China, spring 1994. *Journal American Rhododendron Society* 49:86-88, 103-105.

Cox, Peter. 1997. Plant hunting in the disappearing forests of China. *Journal American Rhododendron Society* 51:35-40.

Cox, Peter. 1999. Plant Exploration in China, fall 1997. *Journal American Rhododendron Society* 53:42-48.

Cox, Peter, 1999. Tibet 1998—plant hunting amid political unrest. *Journal American Rhododendron Society* 53:135-138,141.

Cummins, Pat. 1965. Development of promising hybrid rhododendrons by Bill Whitney of Brinnon, Washington. *Quarterly Bulletin of the American Rhododendron Society* 19:205-209.

Dale, Bill. 1990. Early Canadian rhododendron grower and hybridizer: George Fraser. *Journal American Rhododendron Society* 44:125-129, 176.

Dale, Bill. 1999. George Fraser, his friendship with Joseph Gable and his hybrids. *Journal American Rhododendron Society* 53:75-77.

Davidian, H. H. 1982. *The Rhododendron Species*. vol. I Lepidotes. Portland: Timber Press.

Davidian, H.H. 1989. *The Rhododendron Species*. vol. II Elepidotes. Portland: Timber Press.

Davidian, H.H. 1992. *The Rhododendron Species*. vol. III Elepidotes. Portland: Timber Press.

Davidian, H.H. 1995. *The Rhododendron Species*. vol. IV Azaleas. Portland: Timber Press.

Doleshy, F. L. A native population of *Rhododendron macrophyllum*. *Quarterly Bulletin of the American Rhododendron Society* 17:3-8.

Drew, Leslie and Frank. 1989. Furs, gold and rhododendrons. *Rhododendrons on a Western Shore*. Victoria, BC: Victoria Rhododendron Society.

Foland, Milton. 1974. George D. Grace 189-1974. *Quarterly Bulletin American Rhododendron Society* 28: 155.

Frisbie, Leonard. 1961. *Rhododendron occidentale* survey. *Rhododendron* XI, I: 3-14.

Galle, Fred. 1987. *Azaleas*. Portland, OR: Timber Press.

Graham, Donald G. 1947. Report on the Seattle Rhododendron Show. In *The Rhododendron Yearbook for 1947*, Ed. Robert Moulton Gatke. Portland, OR: American Rhododendron Society. 101-105.

Graham, Donald G. 1954. Endre Ostbo. *Quarterly Bulletin of the American Rhododendron Society* 8:17-19.

Greer, Harold. 1991. Willard W. Thompson. *Journal of the American Rhododendron Society* 45:18-19.

Greig, Mary. 1969. To Nepal and Kashmir. *Quarterly Bulletin of the American Rhododendron Society* 23:6-7.

Grothaus, Molly. 1963. A stroll through the Rudolph Henny garden. *Quarterly Bulletin of the American Rhododendron Society* 17:202-206.

Guttormsen, Bill. 1977. The Greenwood azaleas. *Quarterly Bulletin of the American Rhododendron Society* 31:172-173.

Hacanson, Honoré. 1998. Letters to the editor. *Journal American Rhododendron Society* 52:204-205.

Hacanson, Mrs. Roy, and Fred Robbins. 1971. Lester E. Brandt. *Quarterly Bulletin of the American Rhododendron Society* 25:172-173.

Hacking, Sue Muller, and Chip Muller. 1993. Exploring rhododendron sanctuaries in Sikkim. *Journal American Rhododendron Society* 47:182-188.

Hall, Benjamin D. 1998. DNA changes accompanying the evolution of plant species. *Journal American Rhododendron Society* 52:9-12.

Halligan, Pat. 1997. Red lepidotes. *Journal American Rhododendron Society* 51:25-27.

Hansen, Ruth M. 1963. Rudolph Henny, Editor of the Quarterly Bulletin and his influence upon the A.R.S. *Quarterly Bulletin of the American Rhododendron Society* 17:200-201.

Hansen, Ruth M. 1974. History of the American Rhododendron Society. In *Quarterly Reprints Bulletin of the American Rhododendron Society*, vol. 1, 2 & 3. Portland, OR: Portland Chapter of the American Rhododendron Society. 5-11.

Helm, Henry. 1998. A rhododendron expedition to Sulawesi, Indonesia. *Journal American Rhododendron Society* 52:135-142.

Hendrickson, Dennis. 1993. The untamed western native: *Rhododendron albiflorum*. *Journal American Rhododendron Society* 47:8.

Henny, John. 1995. ARS Charter Members. *Journal American Rhododendron Society* 49:80-81.

Hodgson, Lillian. 1986. The Botanical Garden, University of British Columbia, Vancouver, Canada. *Journal American Rhododendron Society* 40:208-213.

Holland, Stuart. 1989. About Vancouver Island hybridizers. In *Rhododendrons on a Western Shore*. Victoria, BC: Victoria Rhododendron Society.

Hudson, Roy L. 1949. Rhododendrons in Golden Gate Park. In *The Rhododendron Yearbook for 1949*, Ed. Robert Moulton Gatke, Portland, OR: American Rhododendron Society 6-11.

Hudson, Roy L. 1951. The John McLaren Memorial Rhododendron Dell. *Quarterly Bulletin of the American Rhododendron Society* 5:71-73.

Irving, E. and R. Hebda. 1993. Concerning the Origin and distribution of Rhododendrons. *Journal American Rhododendron Society* 47:139-146, 157-162.

Jones, Adele. 1992. A new look at Crystal Springs rhododendron garden. *Journal American Rhododendron Society* 46:150-153.

Justice, Clive 1990. Observations on peninsula Malaysia rhododendrons. *Journal American Rhododendron Society* 44:5-9.

Justice, Clive. 1991. Archibald Menzies and the Discovery of *Rhododendron macrophyllum*. *Journal American Rhododendron Society* 45:127-130.

Lancaster, Ben. 1967. Adventures in rhododendron hybridizing. *Quarterly Bulletin of the American Rhododendron Society* 21:203-211.

Larson, H. L. 1958. Some of my experiences in hybridizing. *Quarterly Bulletin of the American Rhododendron Society* 12:76-77.

Leach, David. 1961. *Rhododendrons of the World*. New York: Charles Scribner's Sons.

Lofthouse, John G. 1987. The Lofthouse propagator. *Journal American Rhododendron Society* 41:76-78.

Long, Edward H. 1963. Rudolph Henny's varieties in California. *Quarterly Bulletin of the American Rhododendron Society* 17:201.

McClintock, Elizabeth. 1961. Two native rhododendron species. *Journal of the California Horticultural Society* 22:62-66.

McCulloch, Steve. 1984. Micropropagation of rhododendrons. *Journal American Rhododendron Society* 38:72-73.

McCullough, Michael A. 1985. Exploring for the western azalea in southern California. *Journal American Rhododendron Society* 39:70-74.

Mitchell, Jeanne. 1994. *Rhododendron* 'Burnaby Centennial'. *Journal American Rhododendron Society* 48:67-68.

Molinari, Paul, and Parker Smith. 1991. Bob Scott: magic of Maddeniis. *Journal American Rhododendron Society* 45:26-29.

Moynier, William. 1992. Vireya rhododendrons for warmer climates. *Journal American Rhododendron Society* 46:26-29, 41.

Muller, Chip, and Keith White. 1996. Over the Doshong La. *Journal American Rhododendron Society* 50:146-153, 160.

Mulligan, Brian O. 1977. *Woody Plants in the University of Washington Arboretum Washington Park*. Seattle, WA: University of Washington.

Nash, Glen. 1992. Nursery entrepreneur Charles Willis Ward, how his garden did grow! *Humboldt Historian* Nov.-Dec.:4-9.

Nelson, Sonja. American hybrids at Washington Park Arboretum. *Journal American Rhododendron Society* 51:126-128.

Ostbo, Endre. 1945. Rhododendrons in the woodland garden. In *The Rhododendron Handbook for 1945*. Portland, OR: American Rhododendron Society, Binfords & Mort.

Ostbo, Endre. 1946. Rhododendron hybrids. In *The Rhododendron Handbook for 1946*. Portland, OR: American Rhododendron Society, Binfords & Mort.

Pearce, Owen. 1972. The Strybing Arboretum. *Quarterly Bulletin of the American Rhododendron Society* 26:12-17.

Peterson, Rick. 1997. The western North American rhododendron species project. *Journal American Rhododendron Society* 51:68.

Phetteplace, Carl. 1963. Rudolph Henny, his life and work. *Quarterly Bulletin of the American Rhododendron Society* 17:196-199.

Phetteplace, Carl. 1992. The life and work of James Barto. *Eugene Chapter Newsletter*. September 1992: 4-5.

Poole, Ketrina. 1988. *John G. Bacher: Oregon's Early Horticulture Enthusiast*. (Unpublished manuscript).

Portland Chapter, American Rhododendron Society. 1970. Ben Lancaster. *Quarterly Bulletin of the American Rhododendron Society* 24:146.

Silver, Jan., Ed. 1995. *Guide to Washington Park Arboretum*. Seattle, WA: University of Washington.

Smith, Britt. 1984. In Memoriam, Hjalmar Larson. *Journal American Rhododendron Society* 38:22.

Smith, Britt. 1991. Sikkim revisited. *Journal American Rhododendron Society* 45:22-25, 58-59.

Smith, Cecil. 1963. Rudolph Henny's breeding objectives and attainments. *Quarterly Bulletin of the American Rhododendron Society* 17:206-207.

Southern California Chapter of the American Rhododendron Society. 1999. Newsletter: Vol. 23, No. 4: 2.

Spady, Herb. 1991. A new look at hardiness ratings. *Journal American Rhododendron Society* 45:143-144.

Sullivan, Peter. 1972. Ten years of vireya rhododendrons at Strybing Arboretum. In *Vireya Rhododendrons, An Anthology of Articles from the Journal of the American Rhododendron Society 1954-1998*, Ed. E. White Smith and Lucie Sorensen-Smith. Portland, OR: Vireya Vine Publications.

Talbot, Ray. 1991. Milton Wildfong. *Journal American Rhododendron Society* 45:19.

Thompson, Orris. 1998. Evergreen azaleas in the Puget Sound region. *Journal American Rhododendron Society* 52:62-68.

Ticknor, Robert L. 1980. Responsibilities of the rhododendron breeder. *Quarterly Bulletin of the American Rhododendron Society* 34:110-111.

Todd, Norman. 1989. 'Mary's Favourite'. In *Rhododendrons on a Western Shore*. Victoria, BC: Victoria Rhododendron Society.

Van Veen, Ted. 1982. Reminiscences of a rhododendron grower. *Journal American Rhododendron Society* 36:96-97.

Van Veen, Ted. 1984. Giants of the past. *Journal American Rhododendron Society* 38:182-187.

Van Veen, Ted. 1986. *Rhododendrons in America*. Portland, OR: Binfords & Mort.

Walker, Milton V. 1962. The American Rhododendron Society Species Project. *Quarterly Bulletin of the American Rhododendron Society* 16:93-94.

Weesjes, Evelyn. 1989. Vancouver Island hybridizers. In *Rhododendrons on a Western Shore*. Victoria, BC: Victoria Rhododendron Society.

Wellingham-Jones, Patricia. 1990. Mendocino Coast Botanical Gardens. *Pacific Horticulture* 51:40-44.

West, Franklin H. 1994. An ARS retrospective. *Journal American Rhododendron Society* 48:79-80; 138-142; 187-192.

West, Franklin H. 1995. An ARS retrospective. *Journal American Rhododendron Society* 49:8-13; 68-75; 144-146, 169, 173.

West, Franklin H. 1996. An ARS retrospective. *Journal American Rhododendron Society* 50:9-12, 46; 68-71, 89, 96; 136-137.

White, Keith, and Bob Zimmermann. 1998. Plant exploration in Tibet, 1997. *Journal American Rhododendron Society* 52:195-202.

Whitehead, Jack. 1945. Rhododendrons at University of California Botanical Gardens. *The Rhododendron Yearbook for 1945*. Portland: American Rhododendron Society.

THE AUTHOR

Sonja Nelson is the editor of the *Journal American Rhododendron Society*. She has a degree in English from Smith College and in journalism from Western Washington University. She spent her childhood in Excelsior, Minnesota, is a Master Gardener, and tends her own garden in Skagit County, Washington.

Nicholas Brown

Stewart

**Dr. Dave Goheen, Dr. Bob Ticknor, Eleanor Stubbs,
Ted Van Veen and Mike Stewart**

THE COMMITTEE

The American Rhododendron Society's Portland, Oregon Chapter chose from its long-time members the following committee to see that this book was written. Their collective years of experience, knowledge and dedication were invaluable in the writting of this publication.

The committee includes: Mike Stewart, Dover Nursery; Ted Van Veen, Van Veen Nursery; Eleanor Stubbs, Stubbs Shrubs; Dr. Dave Goheen, Hybridizer; and Dr. Bob Ticknor, Professor of Horticulture, Oregon State University.